Cursive Handwriting Workbook For Teens

belongs to:

_____

This cursive Handwriting Workbook is divided into the following parts:

Part 1:
Learning the cursive Alphabet:
Trace and practice letters a-z and A-Z

Part 2:
writing three letter words

Part 3:
writing four letter words

Part 4:
writing five letter words

Part 5:
writing words starting with a Capital letter

Part 6:
writing Numbers and Numbers Words 1- 20

Part 7:
Writing sentences and motivational quotes

Part 1:
Learning Letters

Trace the letters and practice writing them in the remaining space

Are you ready ?
Let's go

a	B	C	D	E	F	Z	H	I	g	K	L	M	N	O	P	Q	R	S	T	U	V	W	X	Y	Z

Starting at number 1, trace the letter by following the order of numbered circles

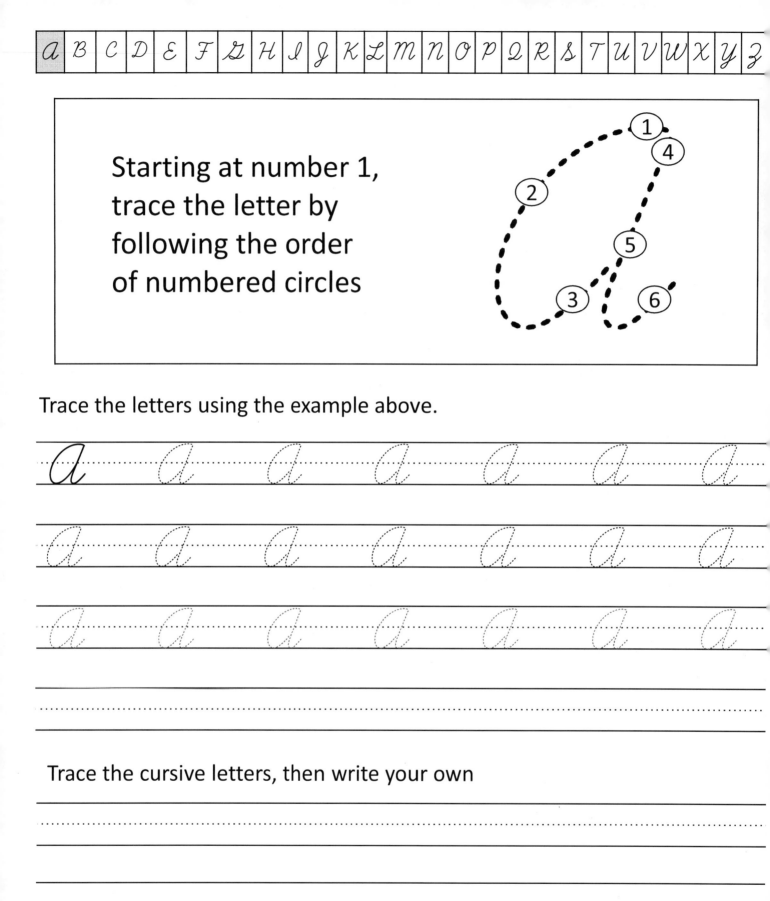

Trace the letters using the example above.

Trace the cursive letters, then write your own

Starting at number 1, trace the letter by following the order of numbered circles

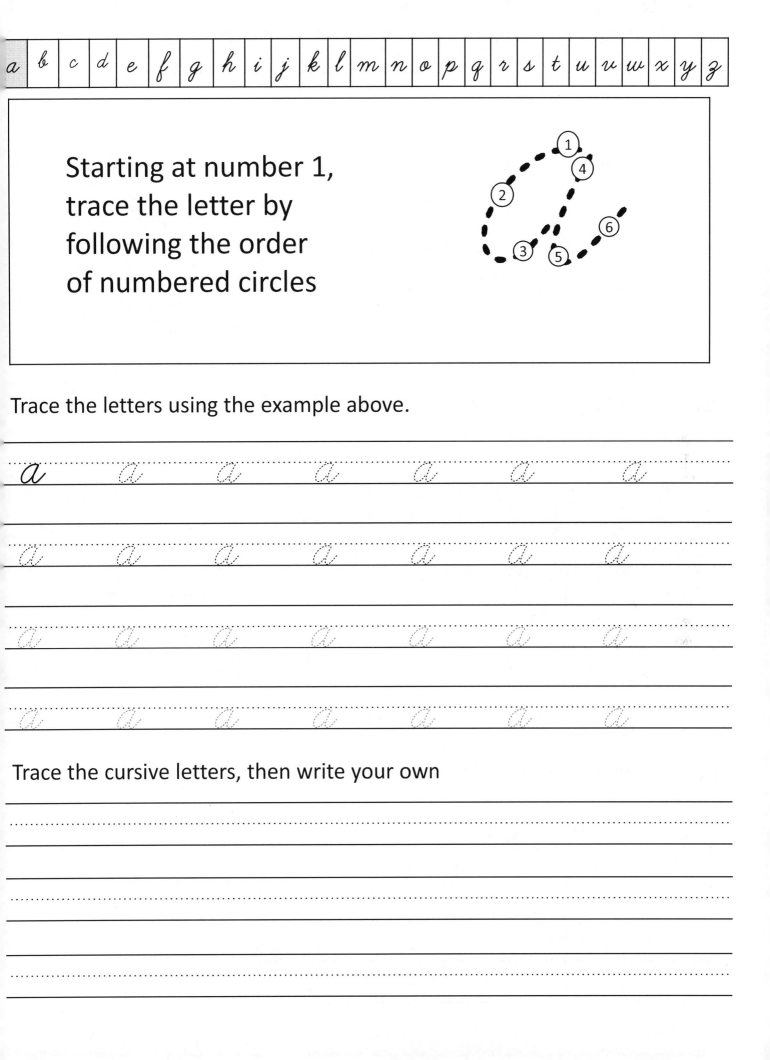

Trace the letters using the example above.

a   a   a   a   a   a   a

a   a   a   a   a   a   a

a   a   a   a   a   a   a

a   a   a   a   a   a   a

Trace the cursive letters, then write your own

Starting at number 1, trace the letter by following the order of numbered circles

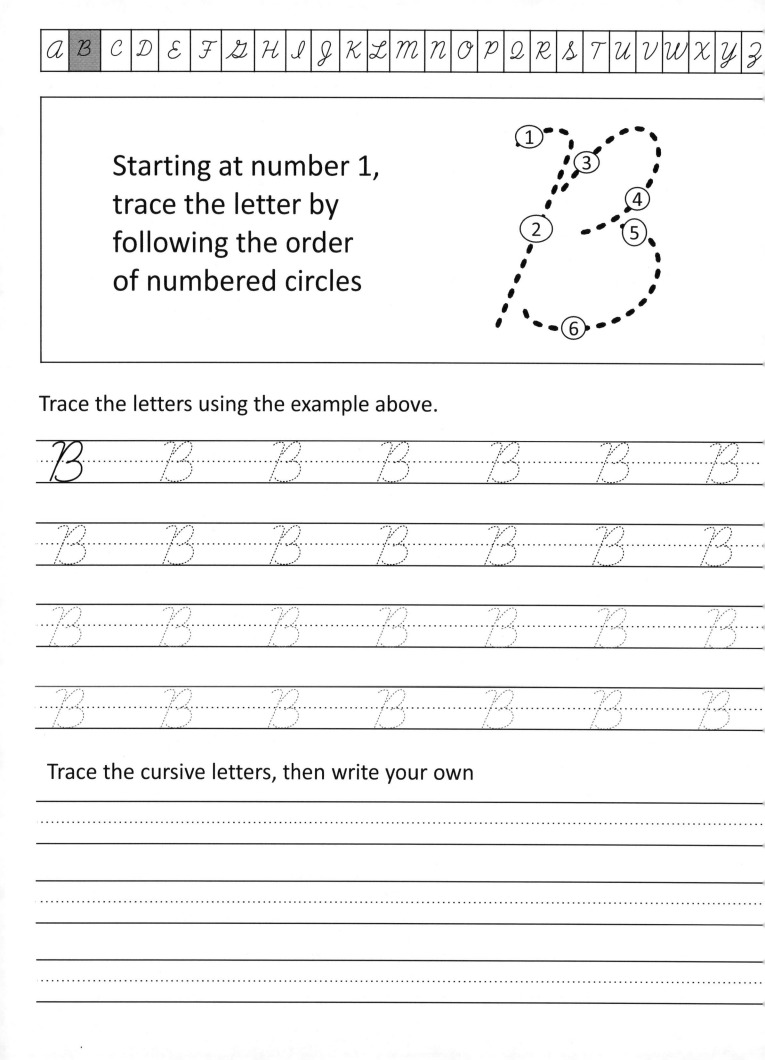

Trace the letters using the example above.

Trace the cursive letters, then write your own

Starting at number 1, trace the letter by following the order of numbered circles

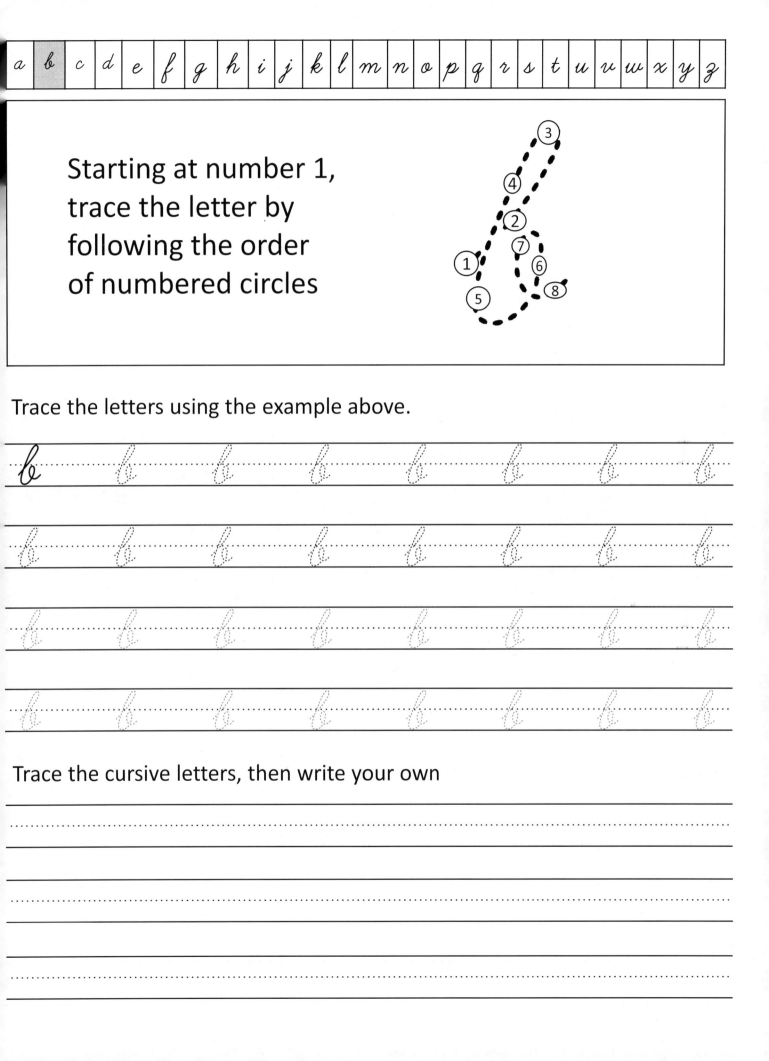

Trace the letters using the example above.

Trace the cursive letters, then write your own

a B C D E F G H I J K L M N O P Q R S T U V W X Y Z

Starting at number 1,
trace the letter by
following the order
of numbered circles

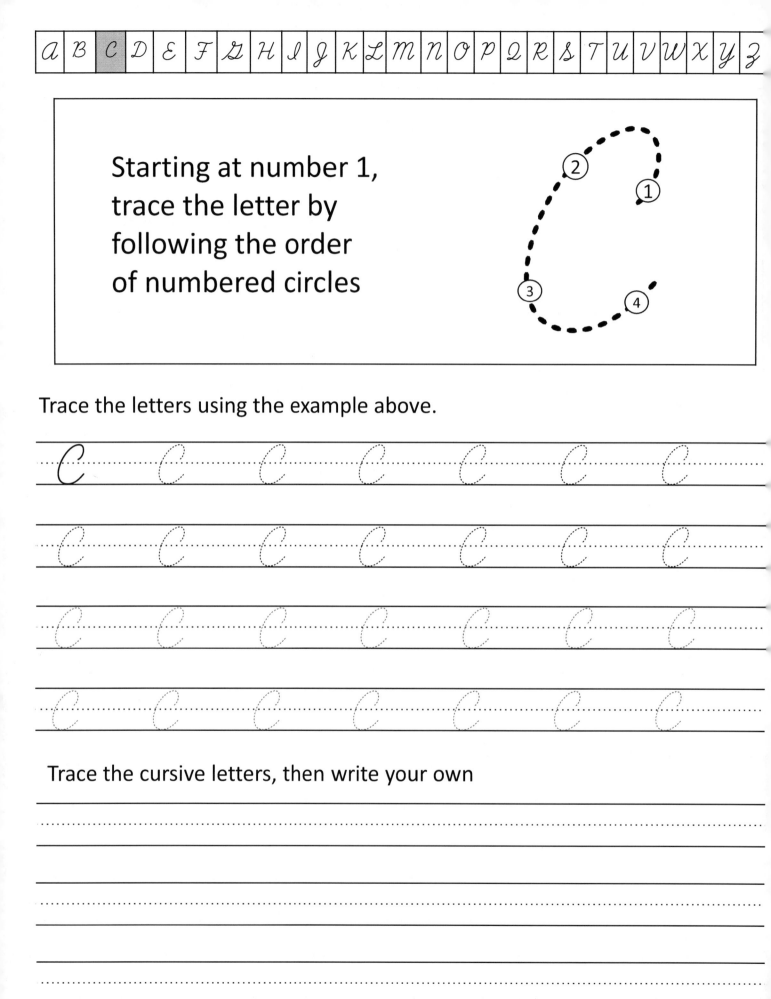

Trace the letters using the example above.

C   C   C   C   C   C   C

C   C   C   C   C   C   C

C   C   C   C   C   C   C

C   C   C   C   C   C   C

Trace the cursive letters, then write your own

Starting at number 1,
trace the letter by
following the order
of numbered circles

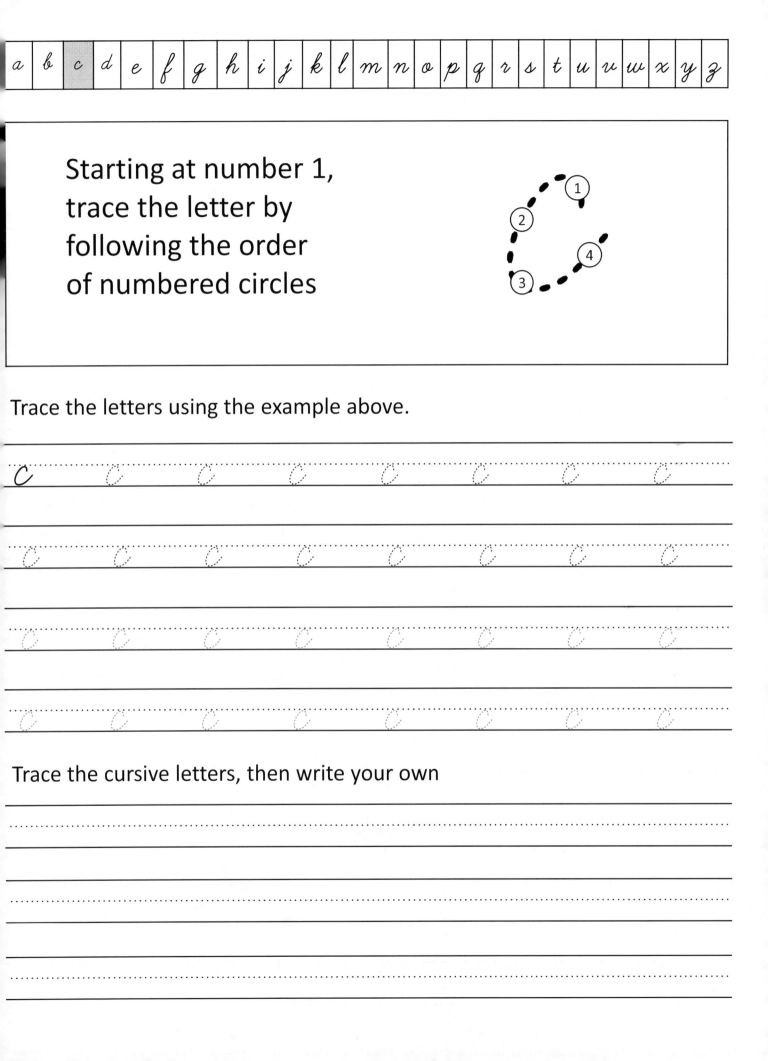

Trace the letters using the example above.

$\mathcal{C}$

Trace the cursive letters, then write your own

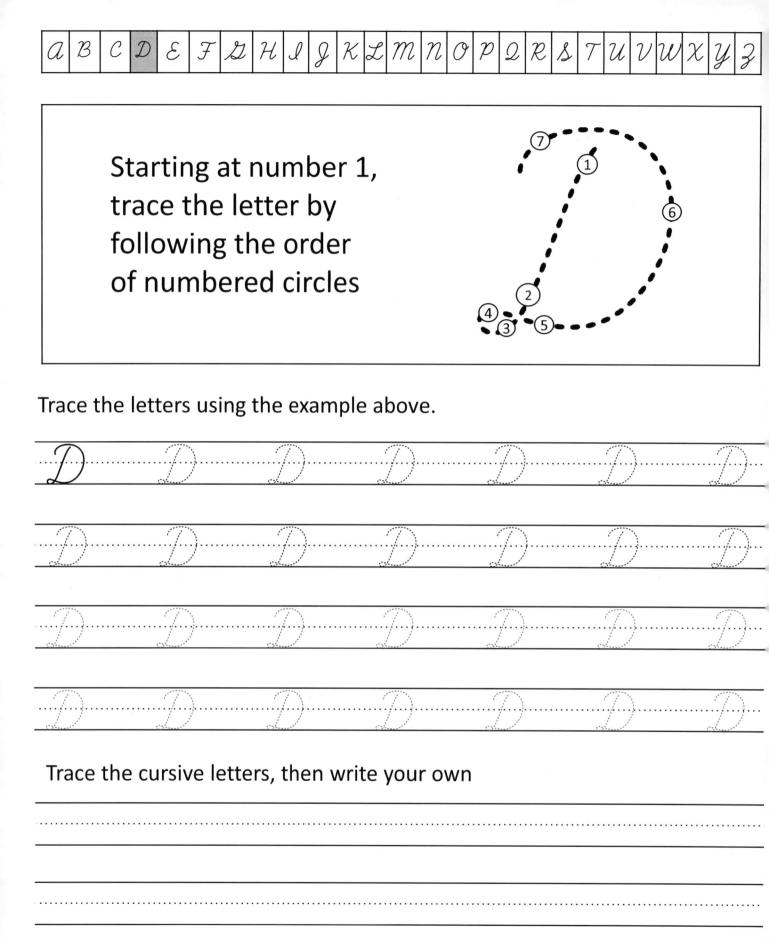

a B C D E F L H I G K L M N O P Q R S T U V W X Y Z

Starting at number 1,
trace the letter by
following the order
of numbered circles

Trace the letters using the example above.

Trace the cursive letters, then write your own

Starting at number 1, trace the letter by following the order of numbered circles

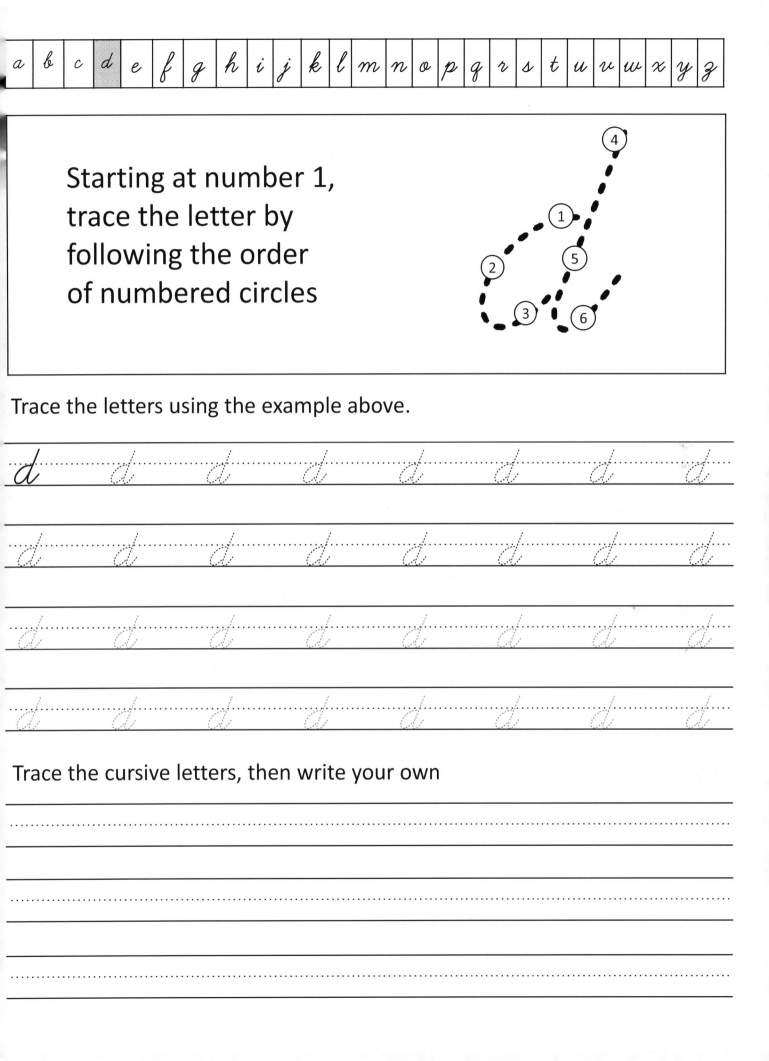

Trace the letters using the example above.

Trace the cursive letters, then write your own

Starting at number 1, trace the letter by following the order of numbered circles

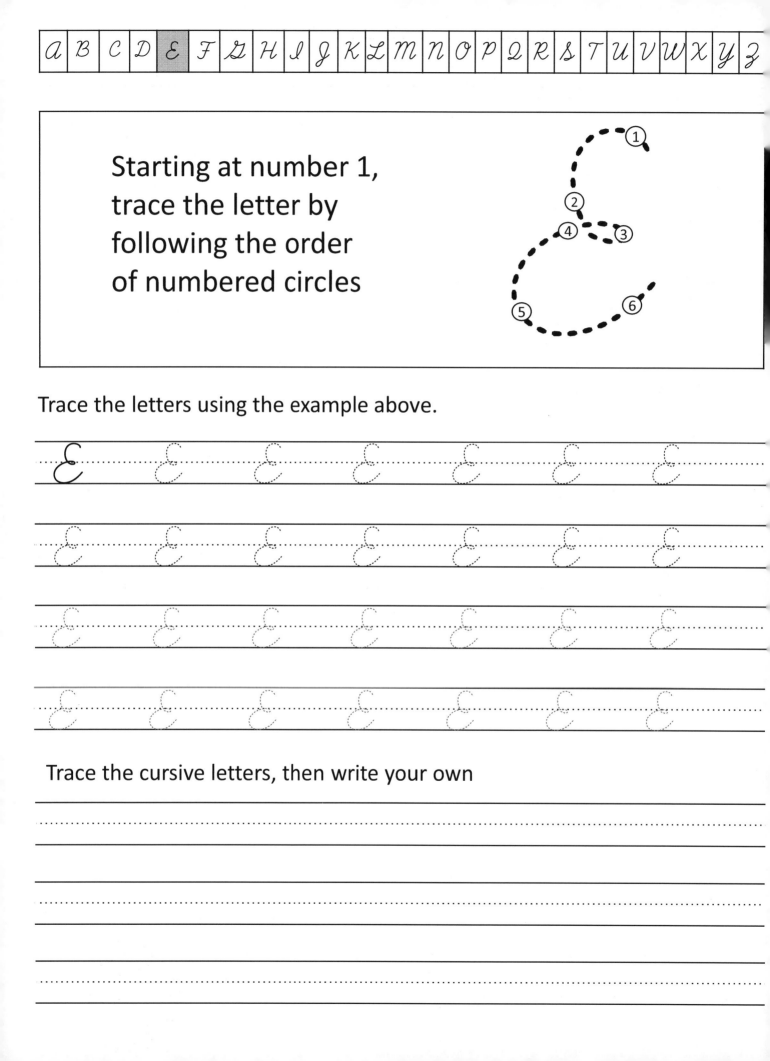

Trace the letters using the example above.

Trace the cursive letters, then write your own

a	b	c	d	e	f	g	h	i	j	k	l	m	n	o	p	q	r	s	t	u	v	w	x	y	z

Starting at number 1, trace the letter by following the order of numbered circles

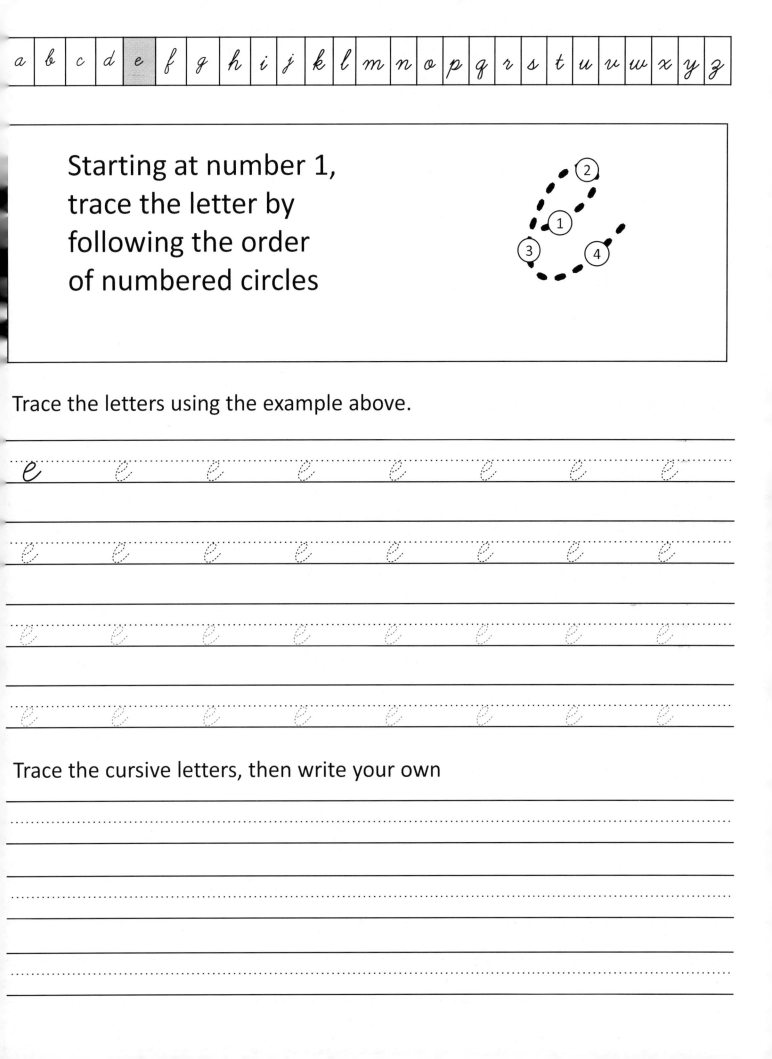

Trace the letters using the example above.

Trace the cursive letters, then write your own

Starting at number 1,
trace the letter by
following the order
of numbered circles

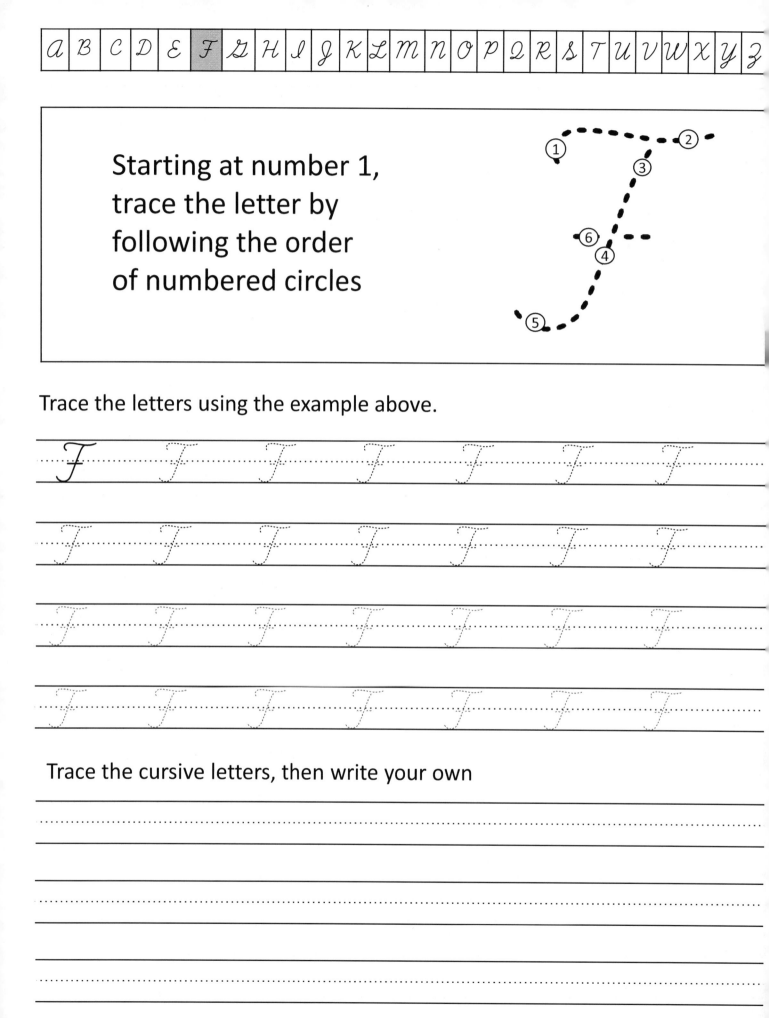

Trace the letters using the example above.

Trace the cursive letters, then write your own

a	*b*	*c*	*d*	*e*	*f*	*g*	*h*	*i*	*j*	*k*	*l*	*m*	*n*	*o*	*p*	*q*	*r*	*s*	*t*	*u*	*v*	*w*	*x*	*y*	*z*

Starting at number 1,
trace the letter by
following the order
of numbered circles

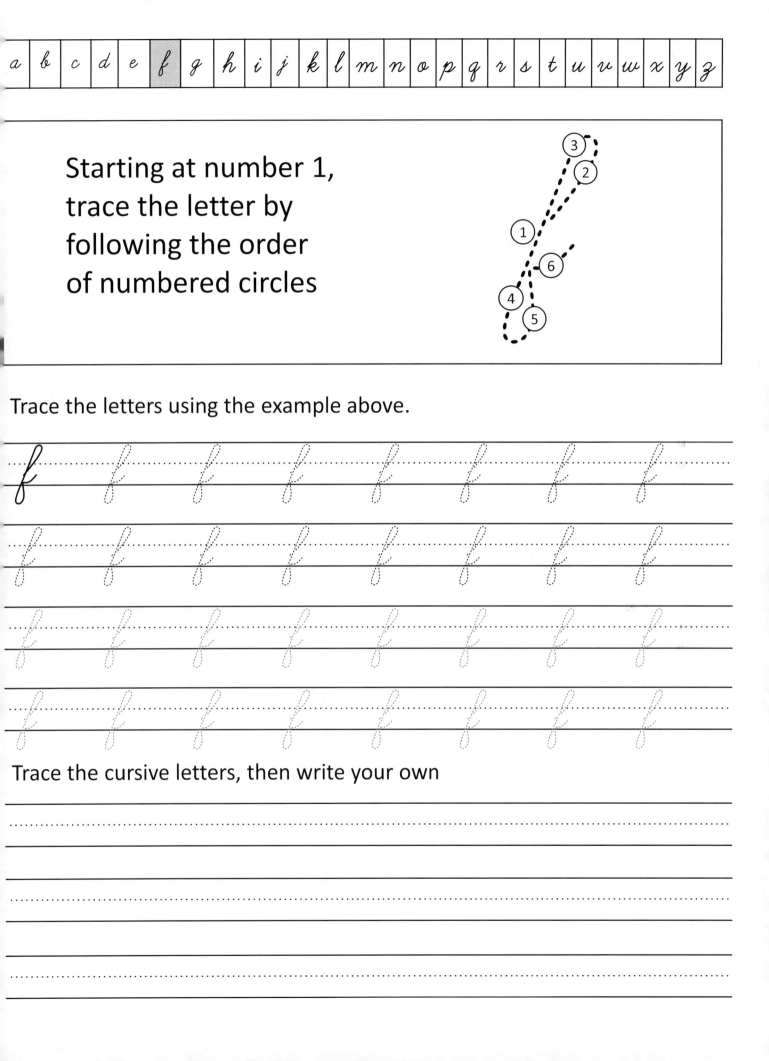

Trace the letters using the example above.

Trace the cursive letters, then write your own

Starting at number 1, trace the letter by following the order of numbered circles

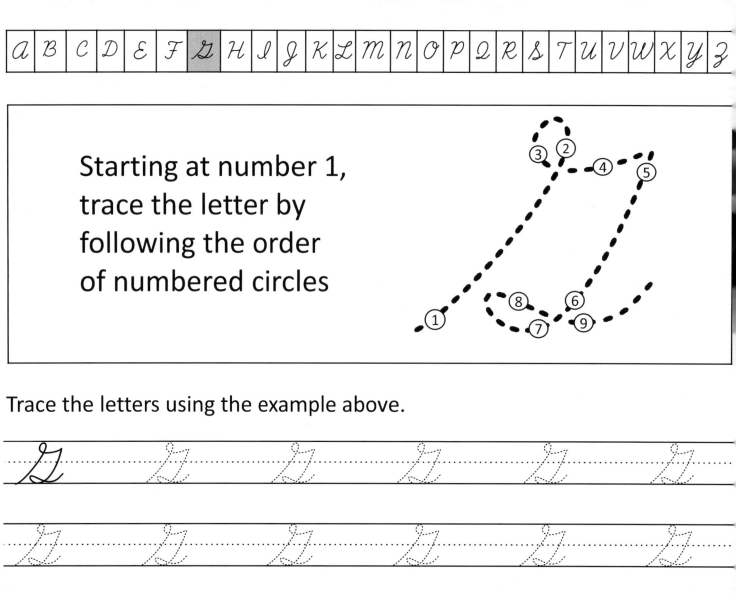

Trace the letters using the example above.

Trace the cursive letters, then write your own

a	b	c	d	e	f	**g**	h	i	j	k	l	m	n	o	p	q	r	s	t	u	v	w	x	y	z

Starting at number 1,
trace the letter by
following the order
of numbered circles

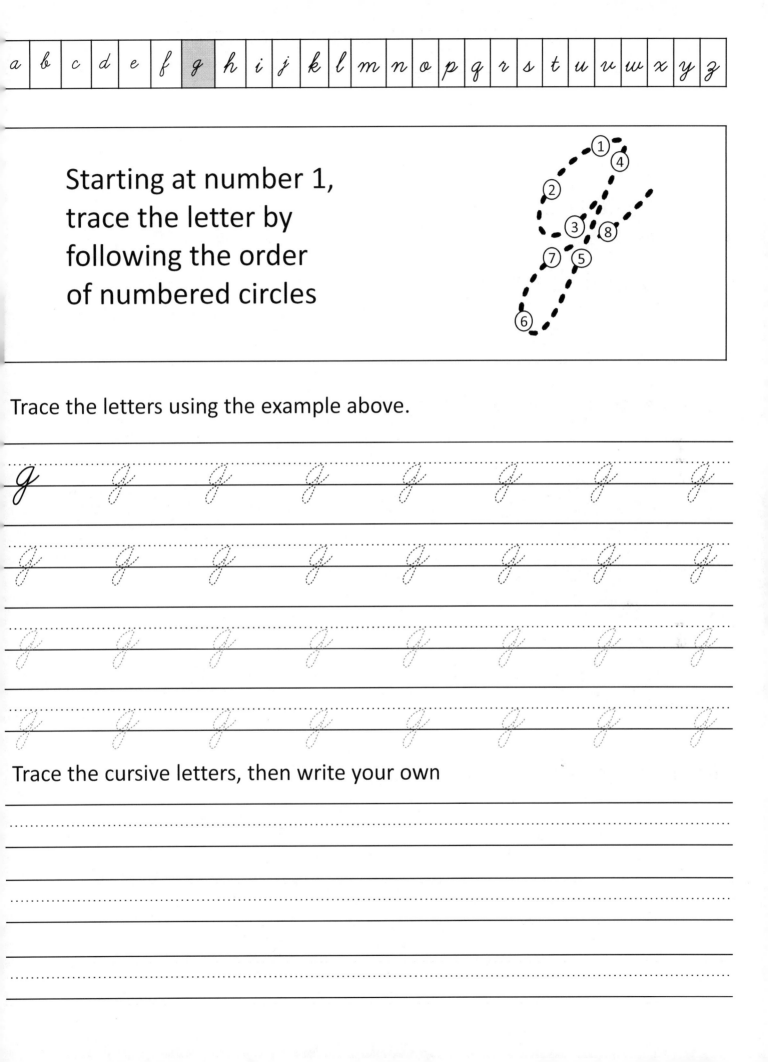

Trace the letters using the example above.

Trace the cursive letters, then write your own

Starting at number 1,
trace the letter by
following the order
of numbered circles

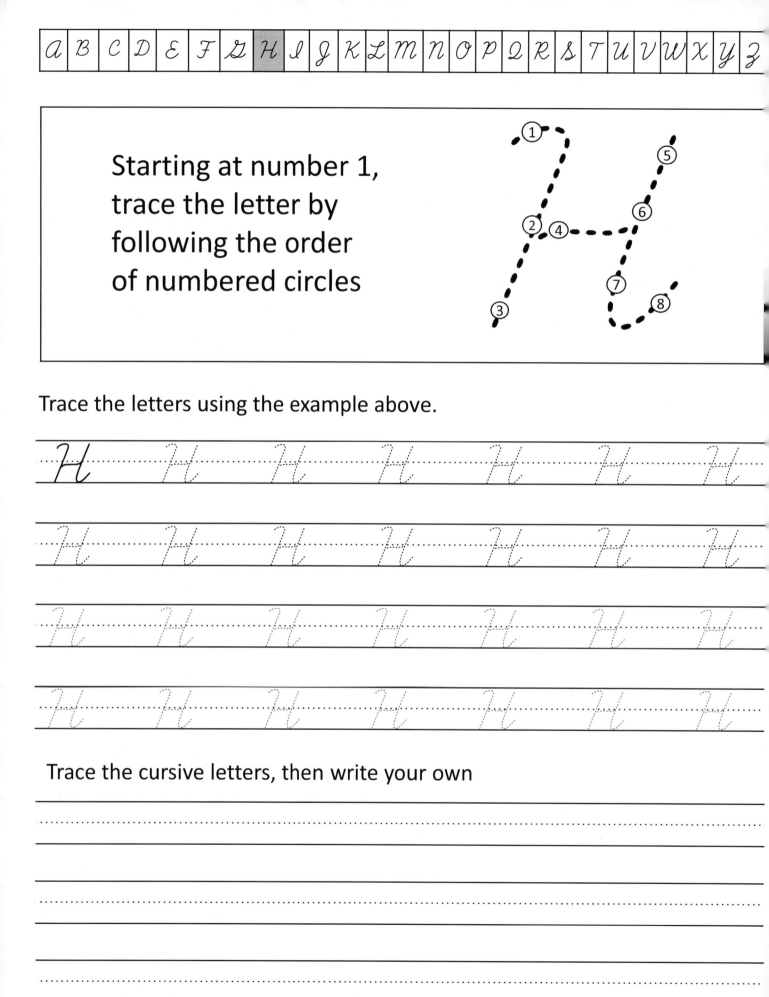

Trace the letters using the example above.

Trace the cursive letters, then write your own

Starting at number 1,
trace the letter by
following the order
of numbered circles

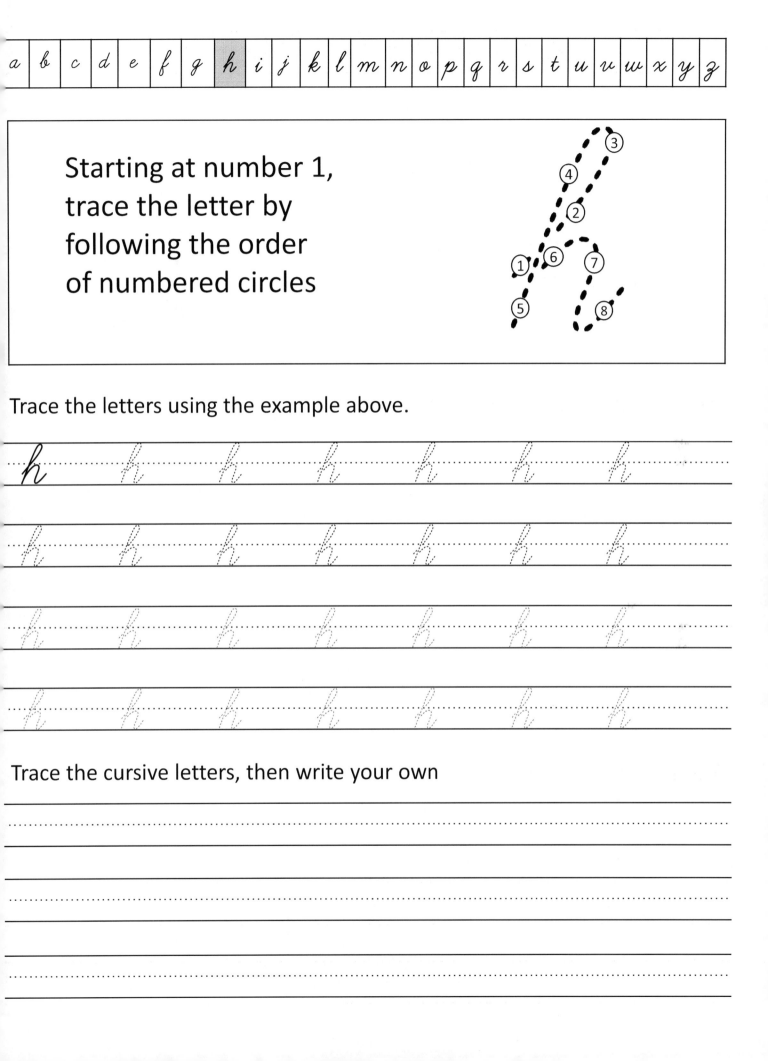

Trace the letters using the example above.

Trace the cursive letters, then write your own

Starting at number 1, trace the letter by following the order of numbered circles

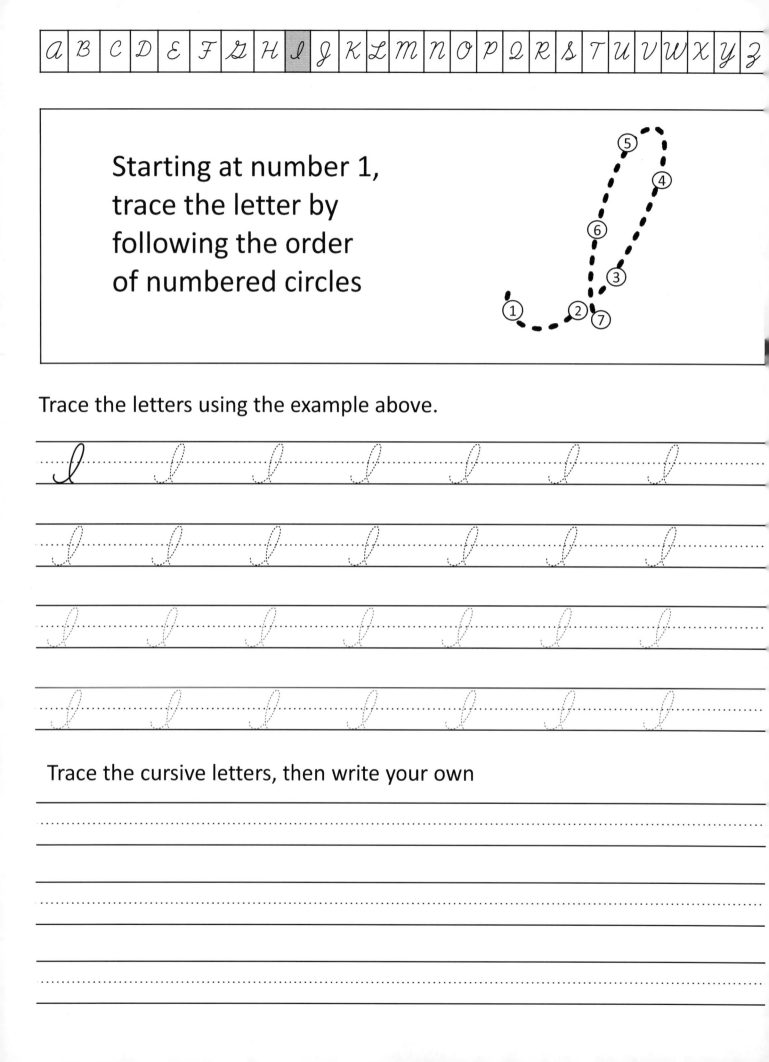

Trace the letters using the example above.

Trace the cursive letters, then write your own

| a | b | c | d | e | f | g | h | i | j | k | l | m | n | o | p | q | r | s | t | u | v | w | x | y | z |

Starting at number 1,
trace the letter by
following the order
of numbered circles

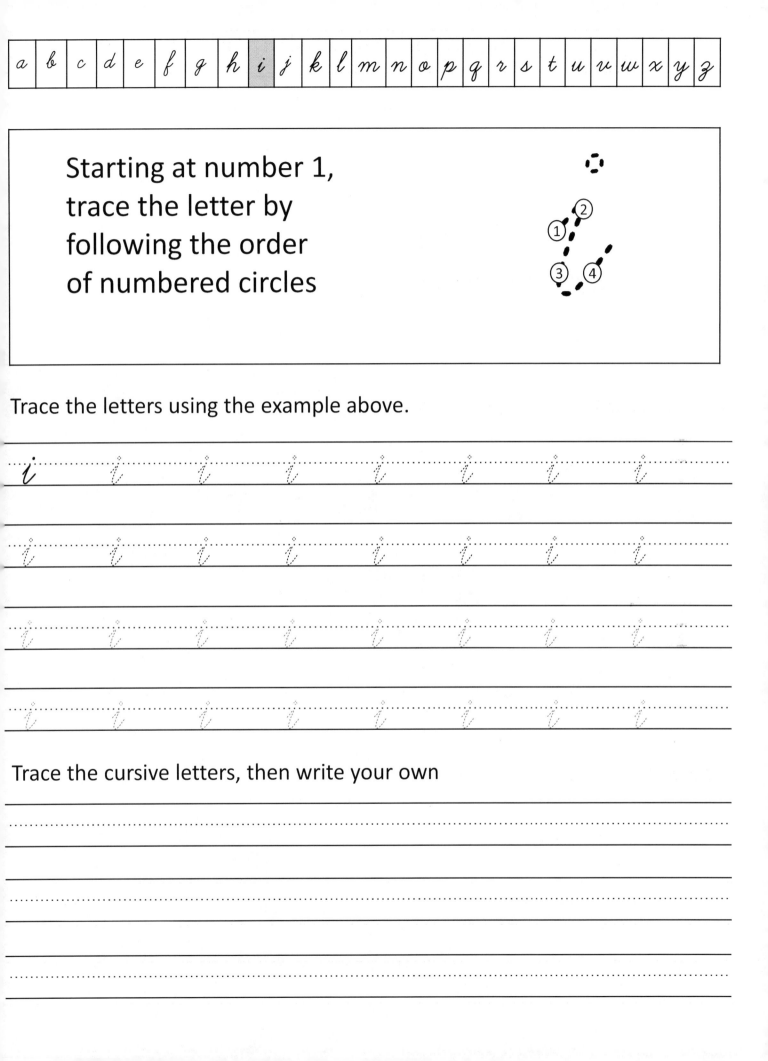

Trace the letters using the example above.

i   i   i   i   i   i   i   i

i   i   i   i   i   i   i   i

i   i   i   i   i   i   i   i

i   i   i   i   i   i   i   i

Trace the cursive letters, then write your own

Starting at number 1,
trace the letter by
following the order
of numbered circles

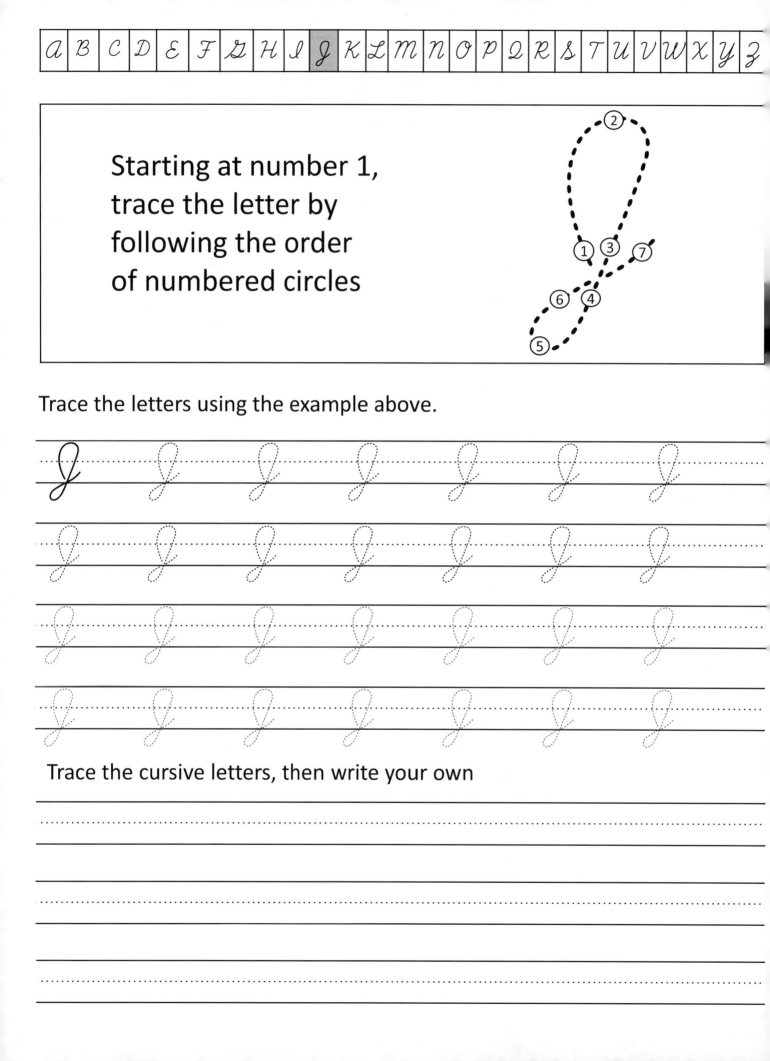

Trace the letters using the example above.

Trace the cursive letters, then write your own

a	b	c	d	e	f	g	h	i	j	k	l	m	n	o	p	q	r	s	t	u	v	w	x	y	z

Starting at number 1,
trace the letter by
following the order
of numbered circles

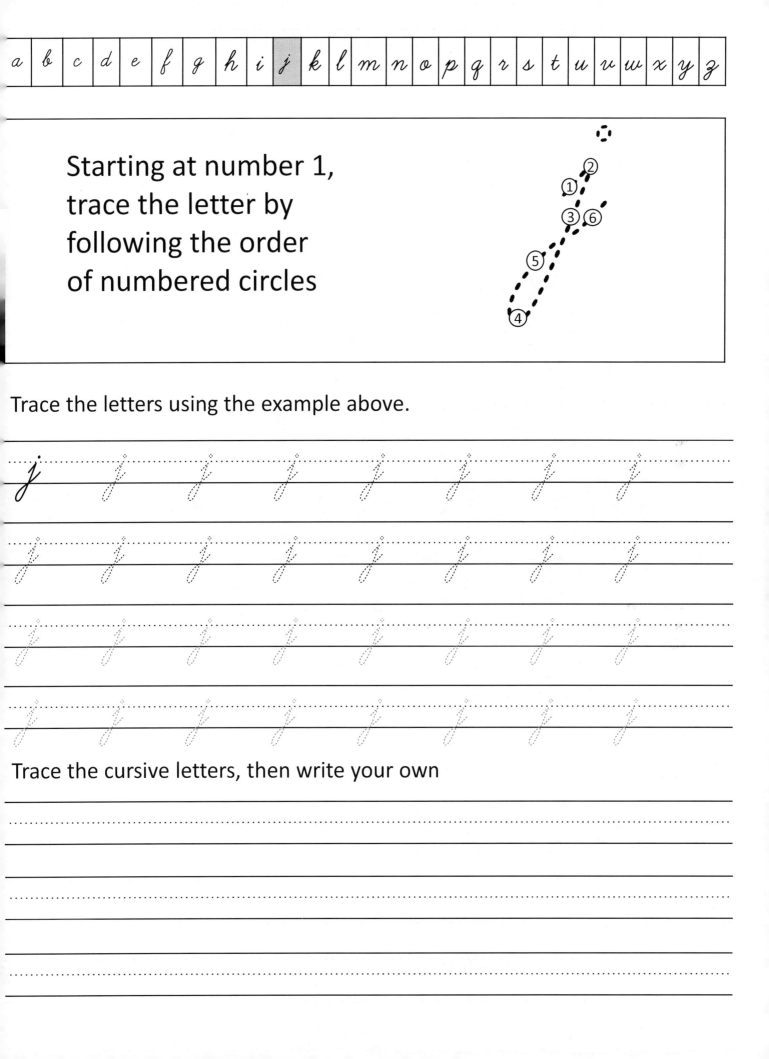

Trace the letters using the example above.

Trace the cursive letters, then write your own

Starting at number 1, trace the letter by following the order of numbered circles

Trace the letters using the example above.

K   K   K   K   K   K   K

K   K   K   K   K   K   K

K   K   K   K   K   K   K

K   K   K   K   K   K   K

Trace the cursive letters, then write your own

Starting at number 1,
trace the letter by
following the order
of numbered circles

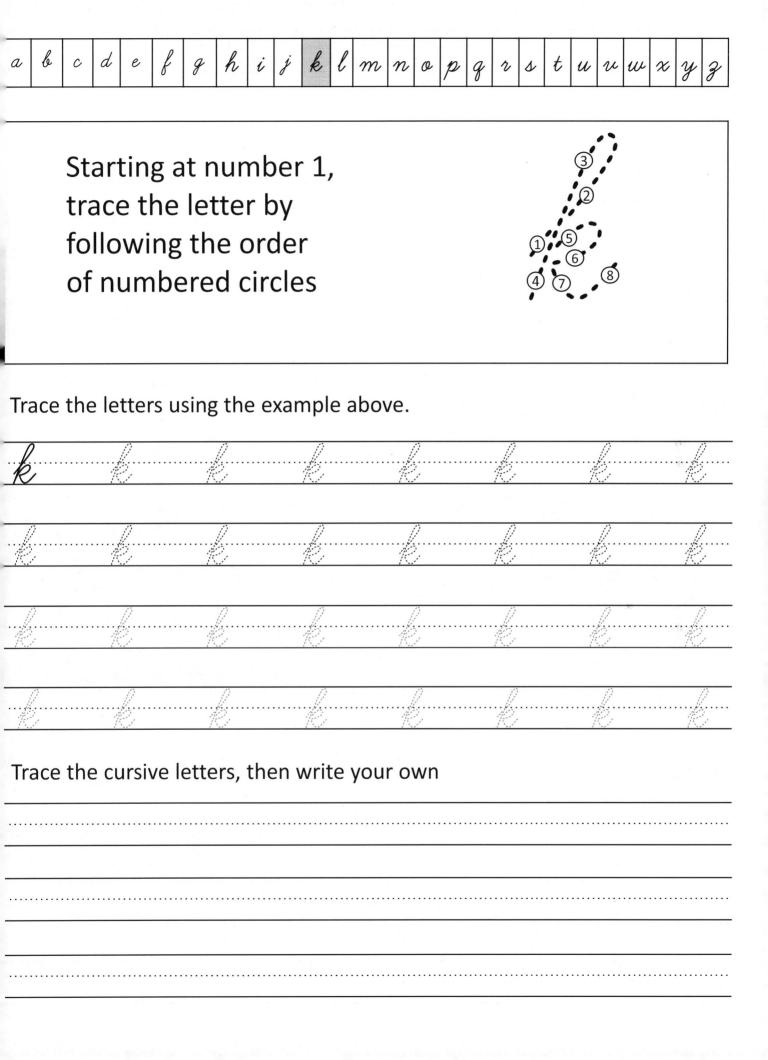

Trace the letters using the example above.

Trace the cursive letters, then write your own

| a | B | C | D | E | F | G | H | I | J | K | L | M | N | O | P | Q | R | S | T | U | V | W | X | Y | Z |

Starting at number 1, trace the letter by following the order of numbered circles

Trace the letters using the example above.

$\mathcal{L}$ $\mathcal{L}$ $\mathcal{L}$ $\mathcal{L}$ $\mathcal{L}$ $\mathcal{L}$ $\mathcal{L}$

$\mathcal{L}$ $\mathcal{L}$ $\mathcal{L}$ $\mathcal{L}$ $\mathcal{L}$ $\mathcal{L}$ $\mathcal{L}$

$\mathcal{L}$ $\mathcal{L}$ $\mathcal{L}$ $\mathcal{L}$ $\mathcal{L}$ $\mathcal{L}$ $\mathcal{L}$

$\mathcal{L}$ $\mathcal{L}$ $\mathcal{L}$ $\mathcal{L}$ $\mathcal{L}$ $\mathcal{L}$ $\mathcal{L}$

Trace the cursive letters, then write your own

Starting at number 1,
trace the letter by
following the order
of numbered circles

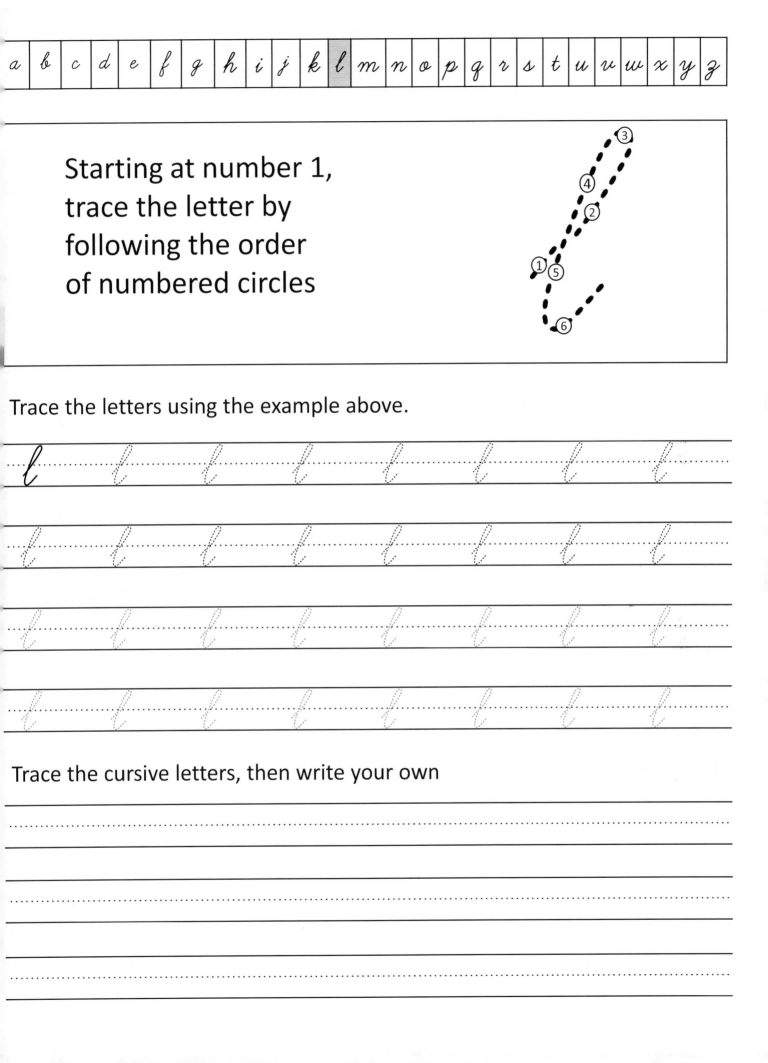

Trace the letters using the example above.

ℓ   ℓ   ℓ   ℓ   ℓ   ℓ   ℓ   ℓ

ℓ   ℓ   ℓ   ℓ   ℓ   ℓ   ℓ

ℓ   ℓ   ℓ   ℓ   ℓ   ℓ   ℓ

ℓ   ℓ   ℓ   ℓ   ℓ   ℓ   ℓ

Trace the cursive letters, then write your own

Starting at number 1, trace the letter by following the order of numbered circles

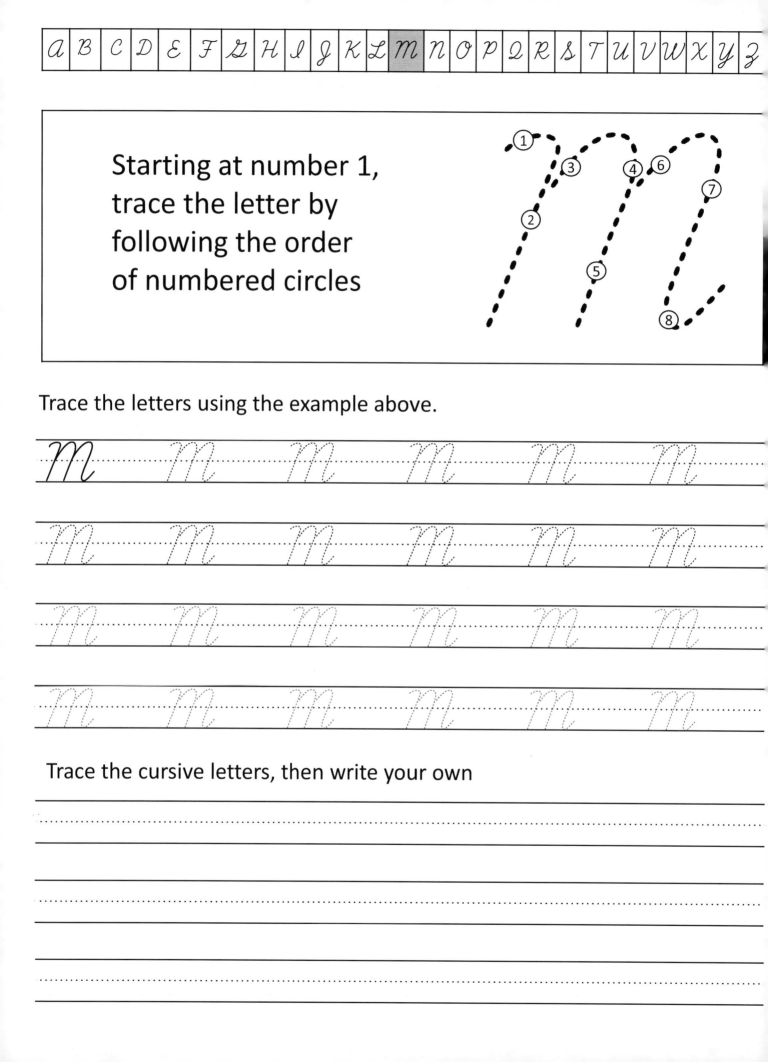

Trace the letters using the example above.

Trace the cursive letters, then write your own

| a | b | c | d | e | f | g | h | i | j | k | l | m | n | o | p | q | r | s | t | u | v | w | x | y | z |

Starting at number 1, trace the letter by following the order of numbered circles

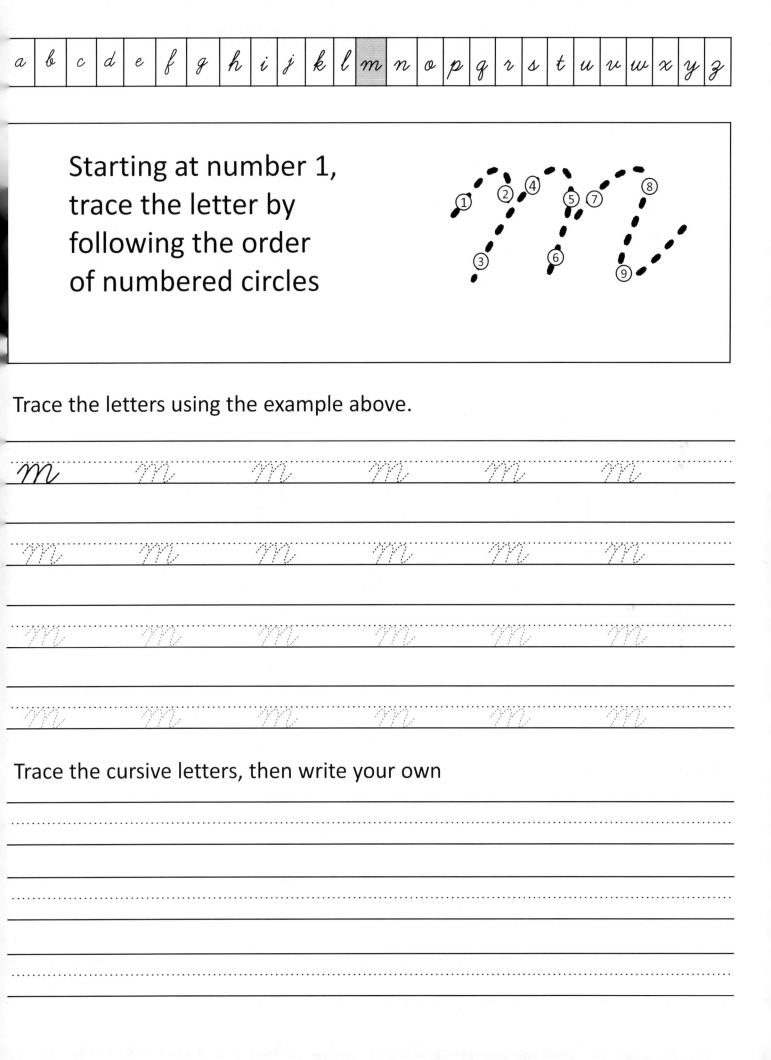

Trace the letters using the example above.

Trace the cursive letters, then write your own

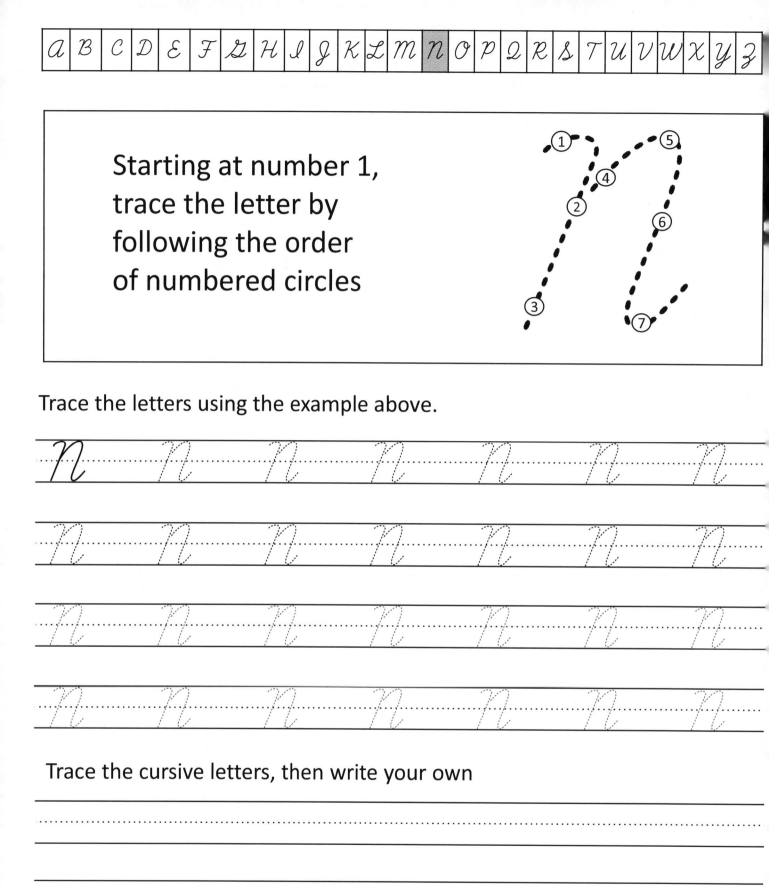

a B C D E F G H I J K L M **N** O P Q R S T U V W X Y Z

Starting at number 1, trace the letter by following the order of numbered circles

Trace the letters using the example above.

Trace the cursive letters, then write your own

Starting at number 1,
trace the letter by
following the order
of numbered circles

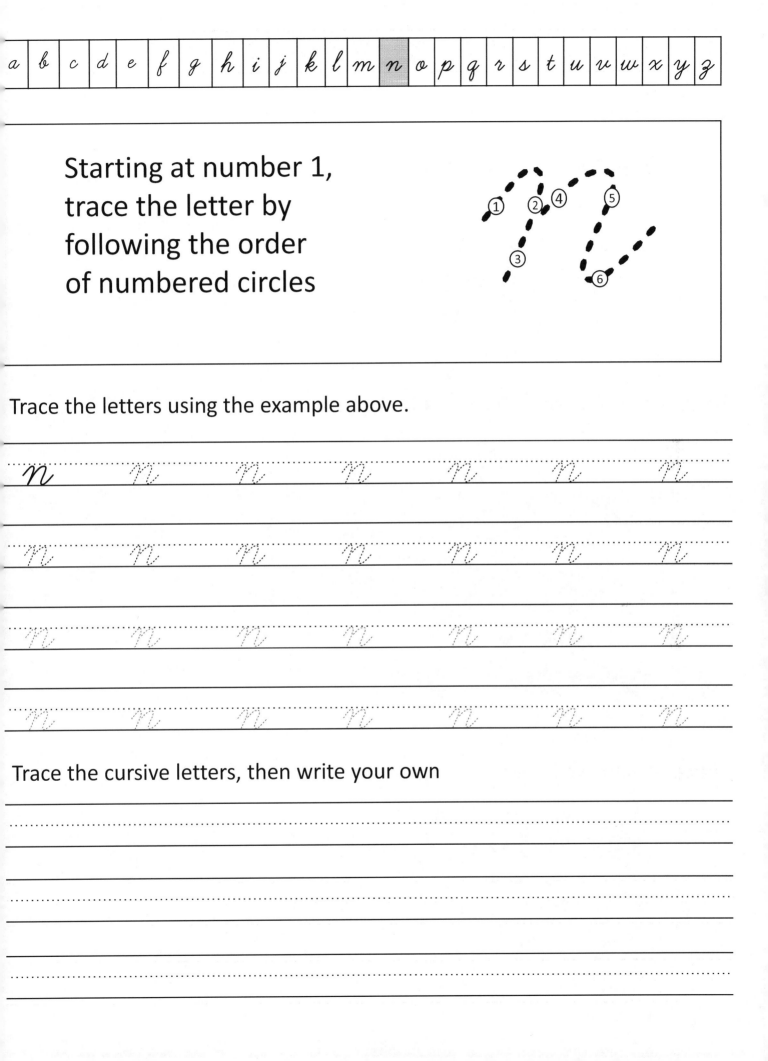

Trace the letters using the example above.

Trace the cursive letters, then write your own

Starting at number 1, trace the letter by following the order of numbered circles

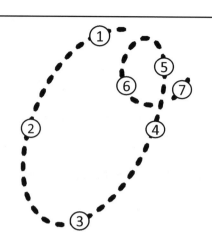

Trace the letters using the example above.

Trace the cursive letters, then write your own

a | b | c | d | e | f | g | h | i | j | k | l | m | n | o | p | q | r | s | t | u | v | w | x | y | z

Starting at number 1,
trace the letter by
following the order
of numbered circles

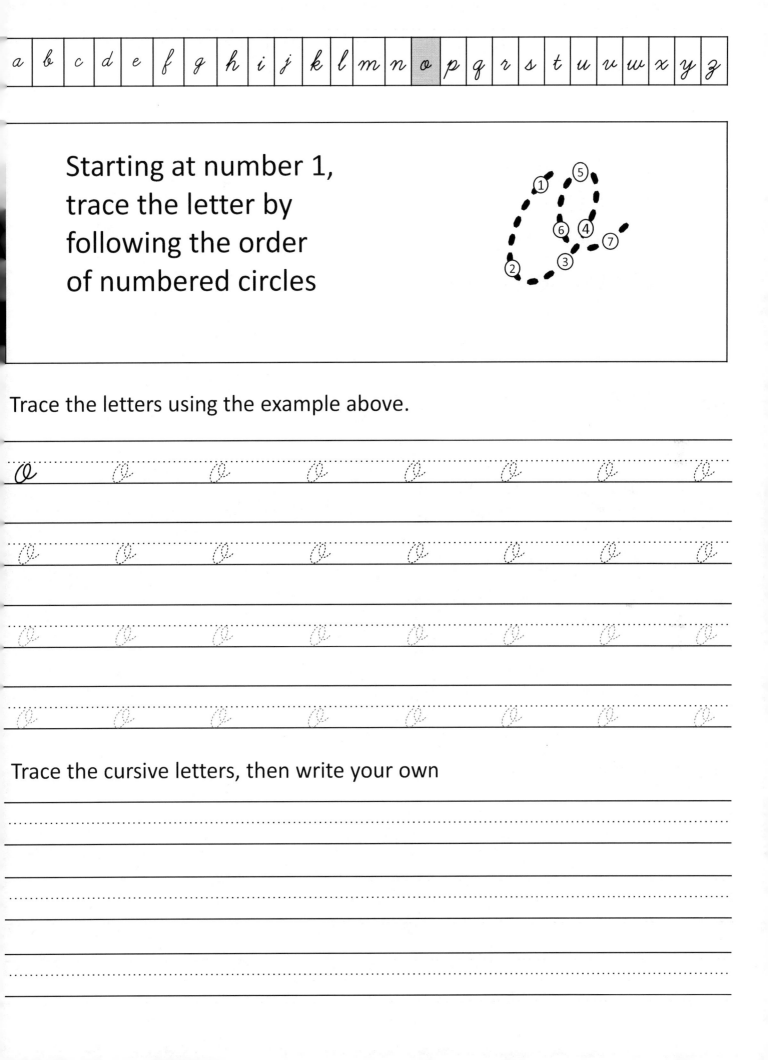

Trace the letters using the example above.

Trace the cursive letters, then write your own

Starting at number 1,
trace the letter by
following the order
of numbered circles

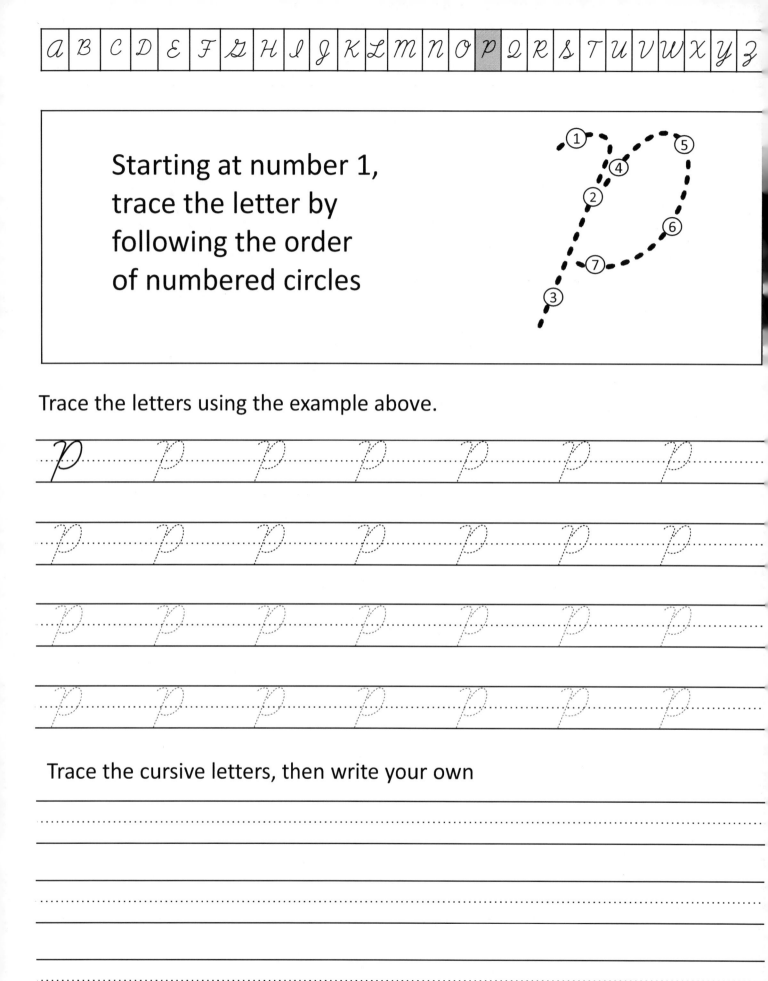

Trace the letters using the example above.

p   p   p   p   p   p   p   p

p   p   p   p   p   p   p

p   p   p   p   p   p   p

p   p   p   p   p   p   p

Trace the cursive letters, then write your own

| a | b | c | d | e | f | g | h | i | j | k | l | m | n | o | p | q | r | s | t | u | v | w | x | y | z |

Starting at number 1, trace the letter by following the order of numbered circles

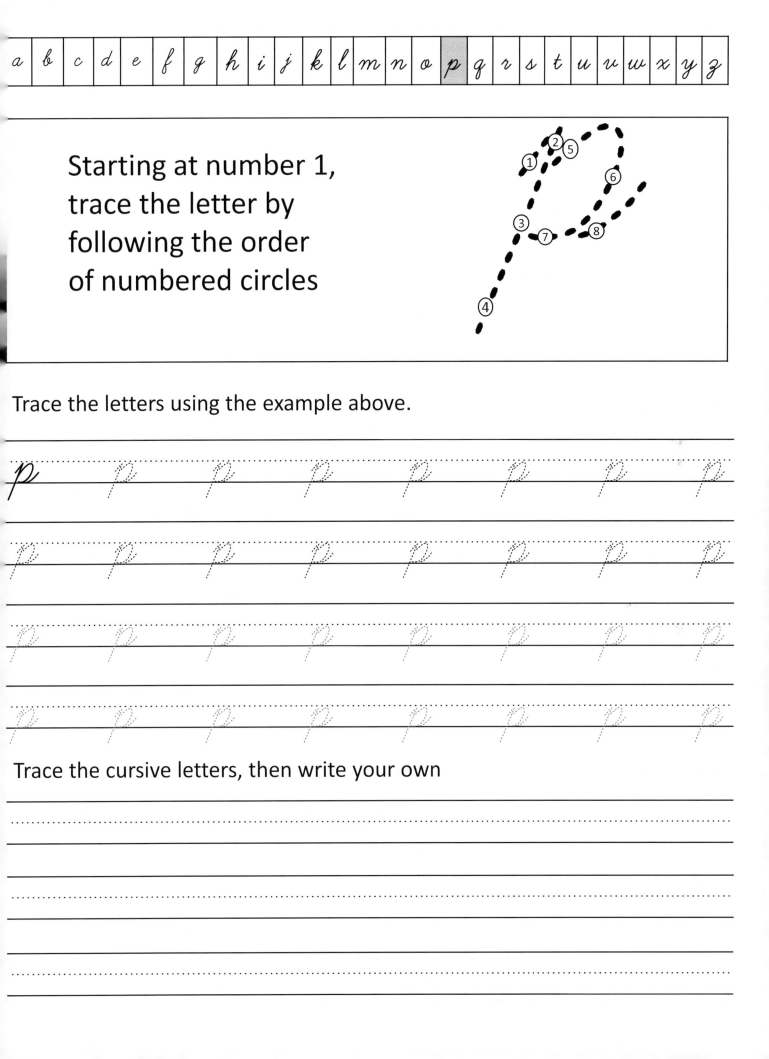

Trace the letters using the example above.

Trace the cursive letters, then write your own

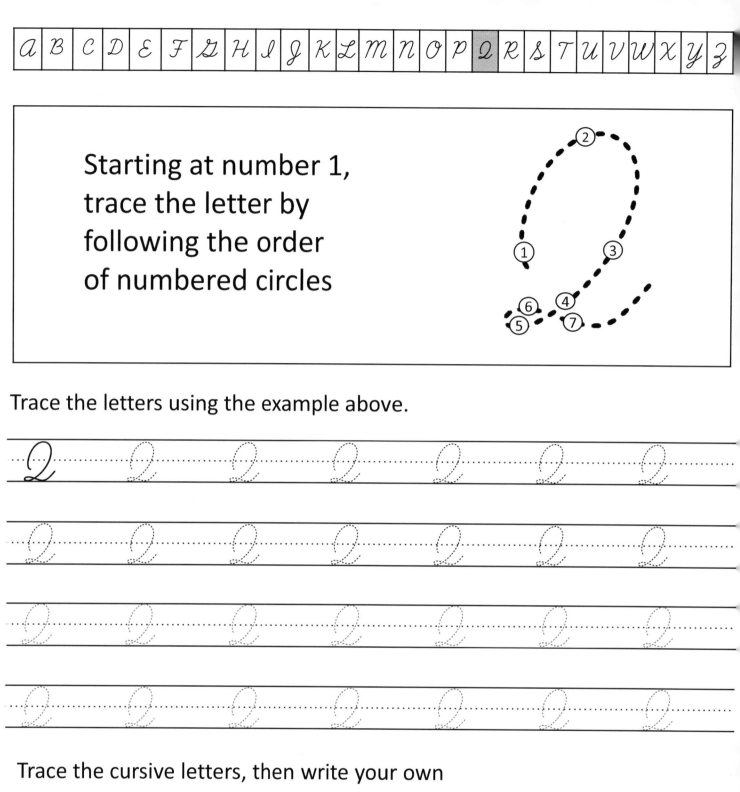

| a | B | C | D | E | F | Z | H | I | g | K | L | M | n | O | P | Q | R | S | T | u | V | W | X | Y | Z |

Starting at number 1,
trace the letter by
following the order
of numbered circles

Trace the letters using the example above.

Trace the cursive letters, then write your own

Starting at number 1, trace the letter by following the order of numbered circles

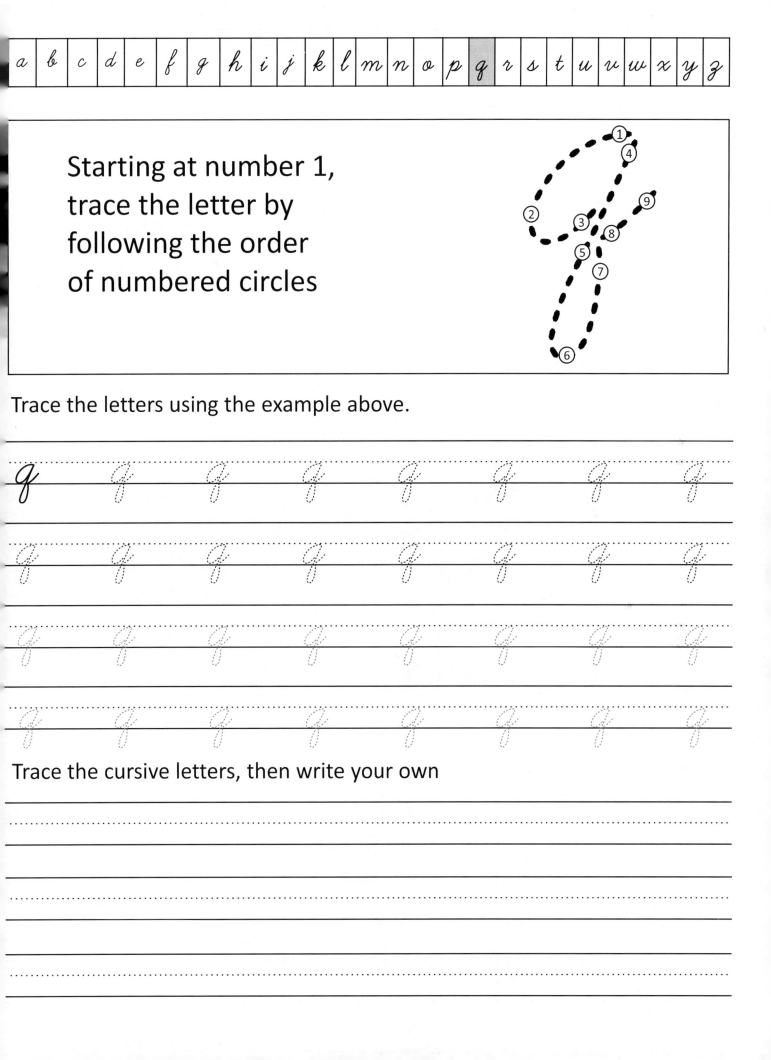

Trace the letters using the example above.

Trace the cursive letters, then write your own

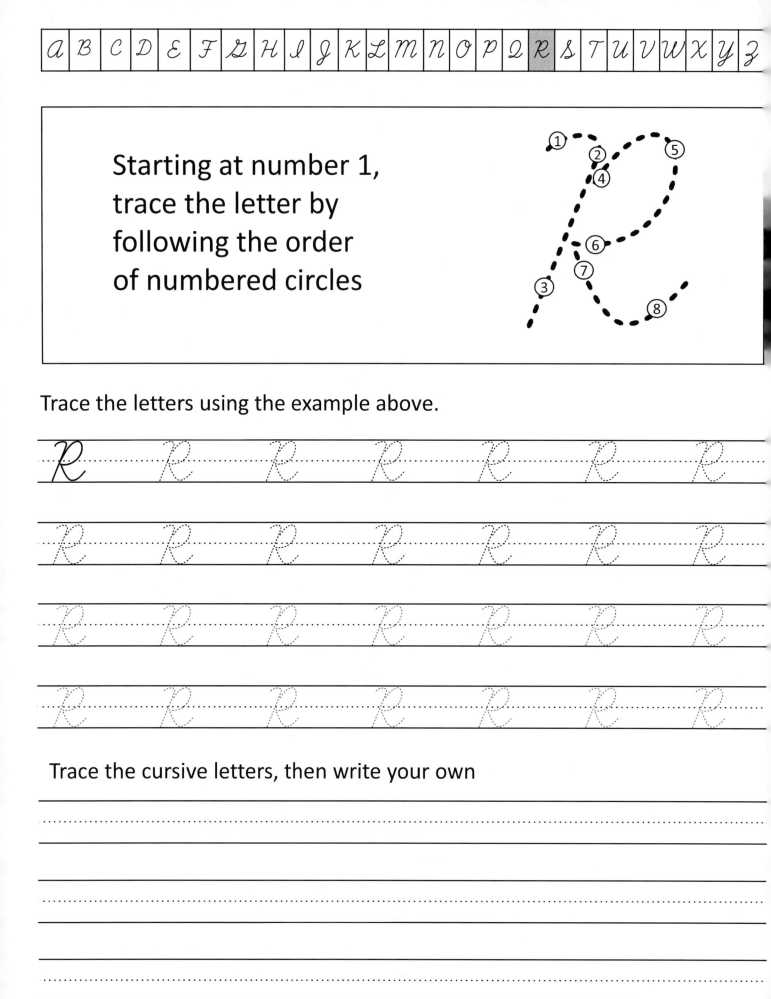

a B C D E F G H I J K L M N O P Q R S T U V W X Y Z

Starting at number 1,
trace the letter by
following the order
of numbered circles

Trace the letters using the example above.

Trace the cursive letters, then write your own

| a | b | c | d | e | f | g | h | i | j | k | l | m | n | o | p | q | r | s | t | u | v | w | x | y | z |

Starting at number 1,
trace the letter by
following the order
of numbered circles

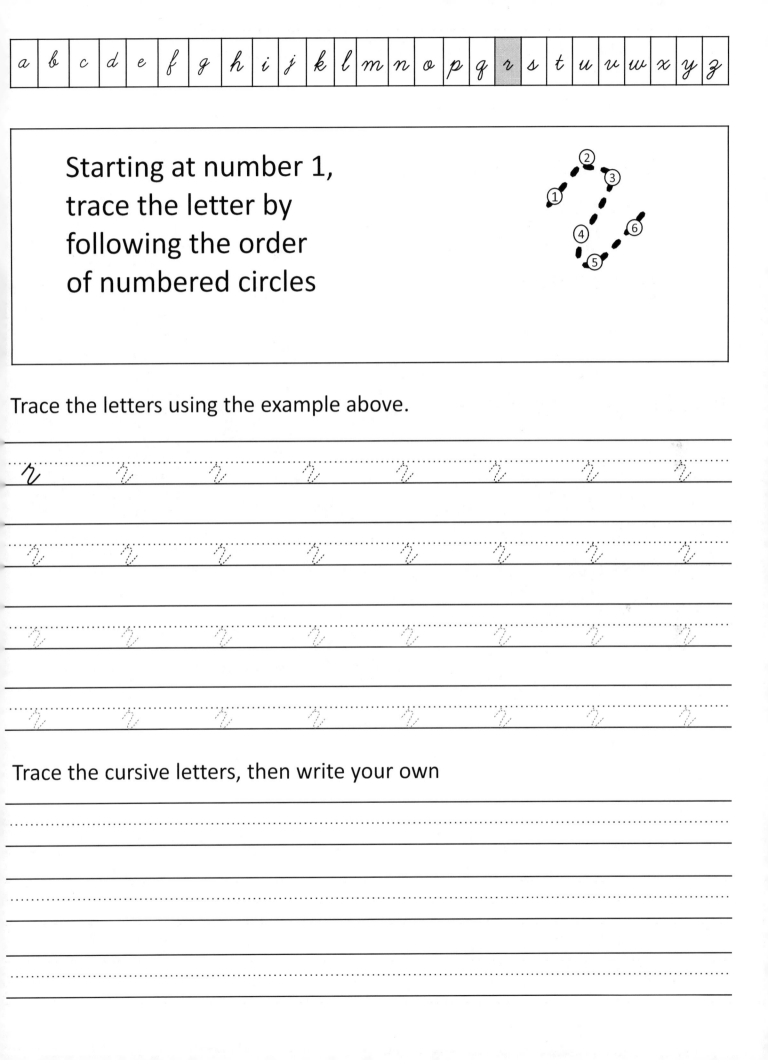

Trace the letters using the example above.

Trace the cursive letters, then write your own

Starting at number 1, trace the letter by following the order of numbered circles

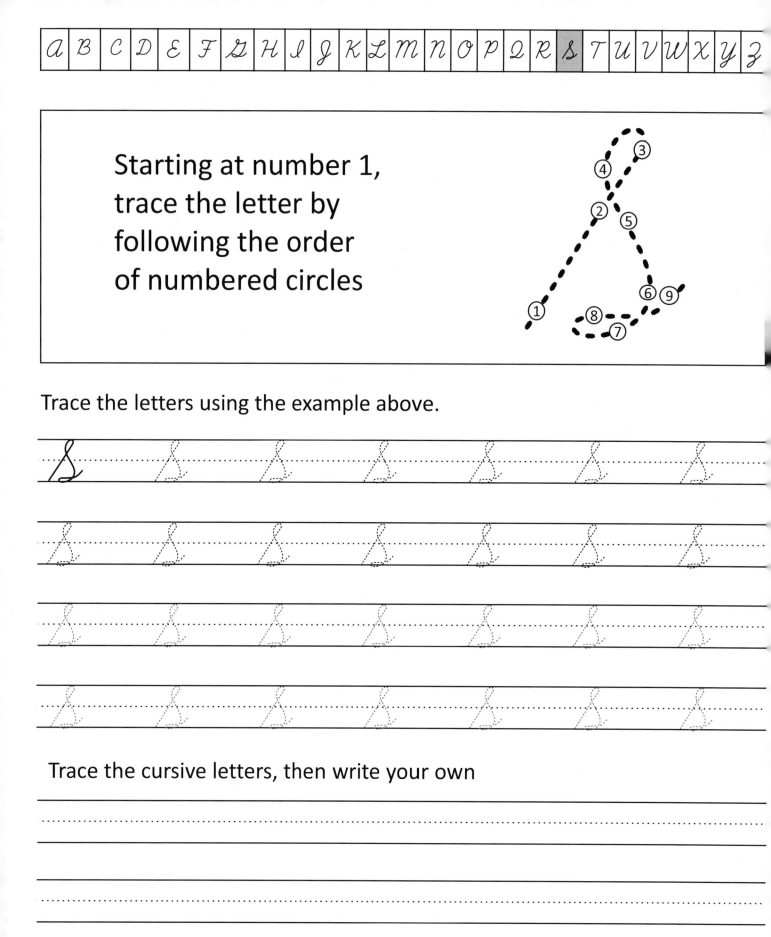

Trace the letters using the example above.

Trace the cursive letters, then write your own

a	b	c	d	e	f	g	h	i	j	k	l	m	n	o	p	q	r	s	t	u	v	w	x	y	z

Starting at number 1,
trace the letter by
following the order
of numbered circles

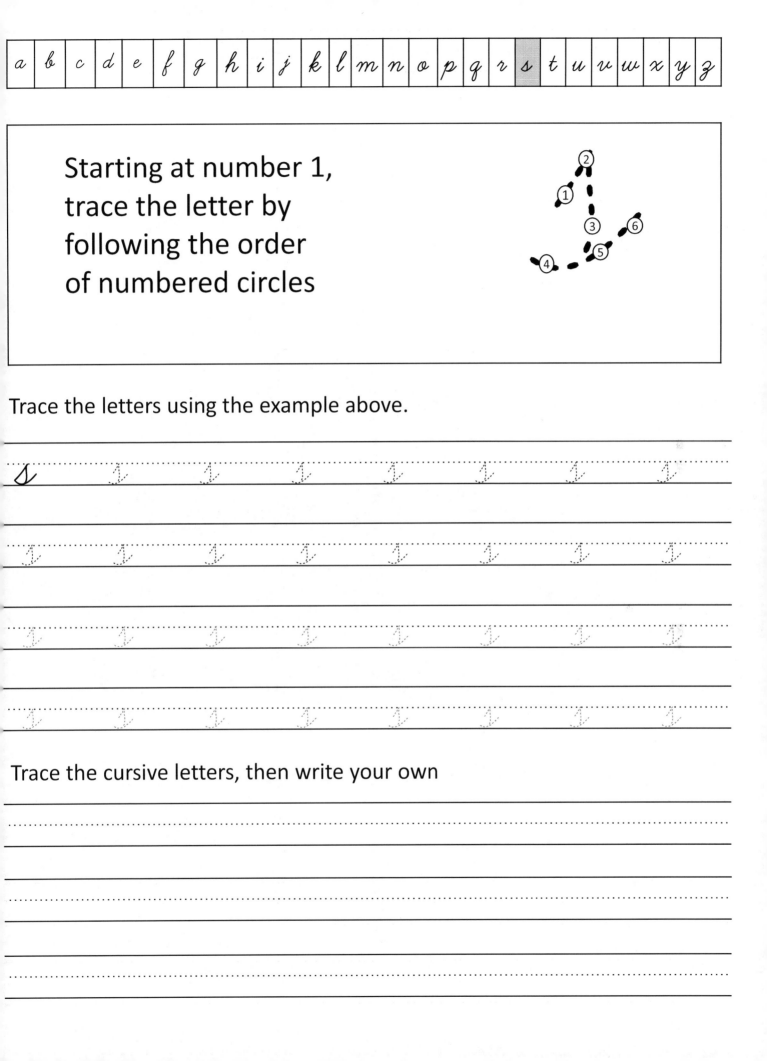

Trace the letters using the example above.

Trace the cursive letters, then write your own

a B C D E F L H I J K L M N O P Q R S **T** U V W X Y Z

Starting at number 1,
trace the letter by
following the order
of numbered circles

Trace the letters using the example above.

Trace the cursive letters, then write your own

Starting at number 1,
trace the letter by
following the order
of numbered circles

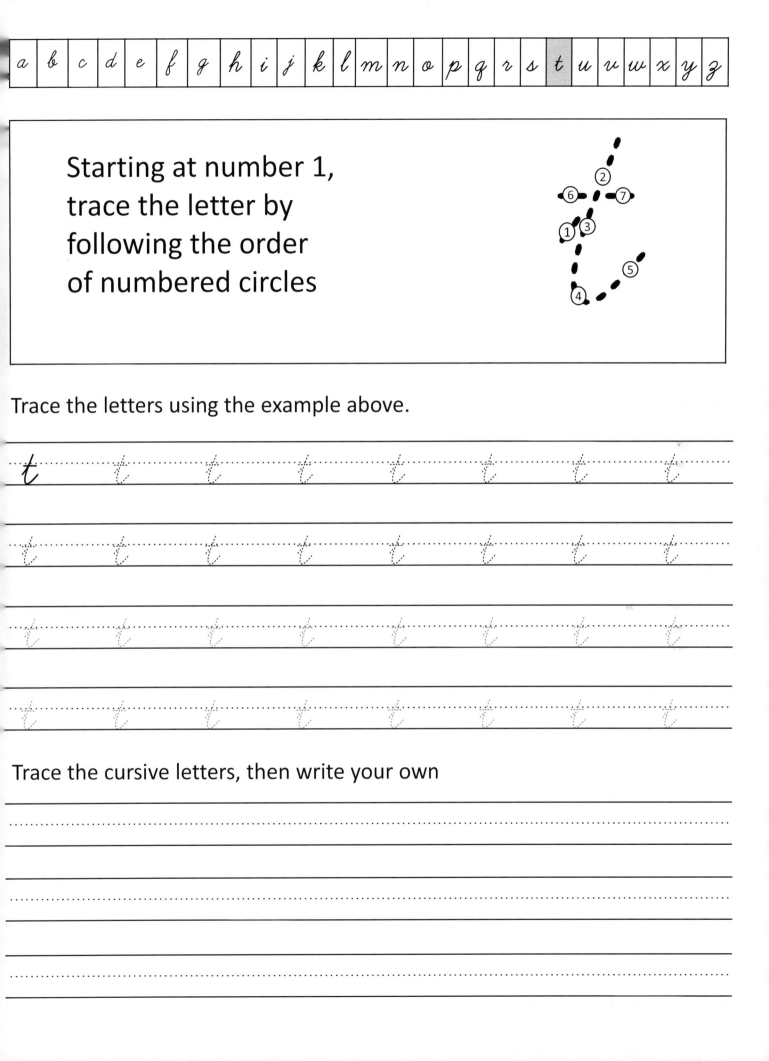

Trace the letters using the example above.

t   t   t   t   t   t   t   t

t   t   t   t   t   t   t   t

t   t   t   t   t   t   t   t

t   t   t   t   t   t   t   t

Trace the cursive letters, then write your own

Starting at number 1, trace the letter by following the order of numbered circles

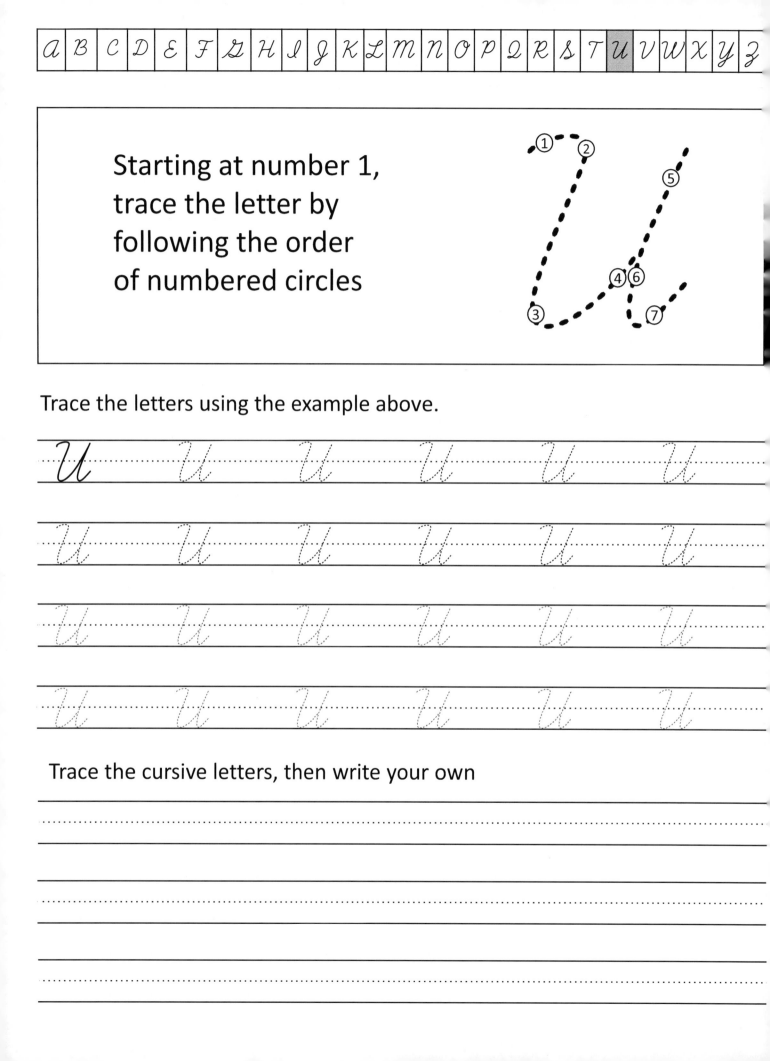

Trace the letters using the example above.

Trace the cursive letters, then write your own

a b c d e f g h i j k l m n o p q r s t u v w x y z

Starting at number 1,
trace the letter by
following the order
of numbered circles

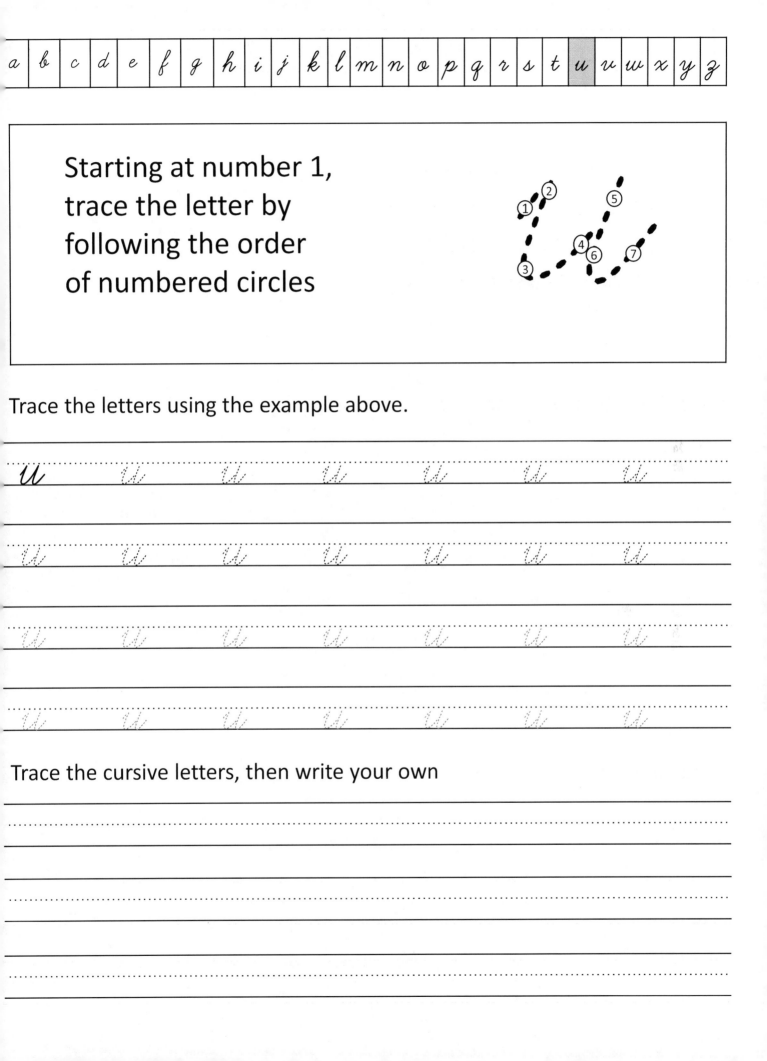

Trace the letters using the example above.

u   u   u   u   u   u   u

u   u   u   u   u   u   u

u   u   u   u   u   u   u

u   u   u   u   u   u   u

Trace the cursive letters, then write your own

| a | B | C | D | E | F | G | H | I | J | K | L | M | N | O | P | Q | R | S | T | U | V | W | X | Y | Z |

Starting at number 1,
trace the letter by
following the order
of numbered circles

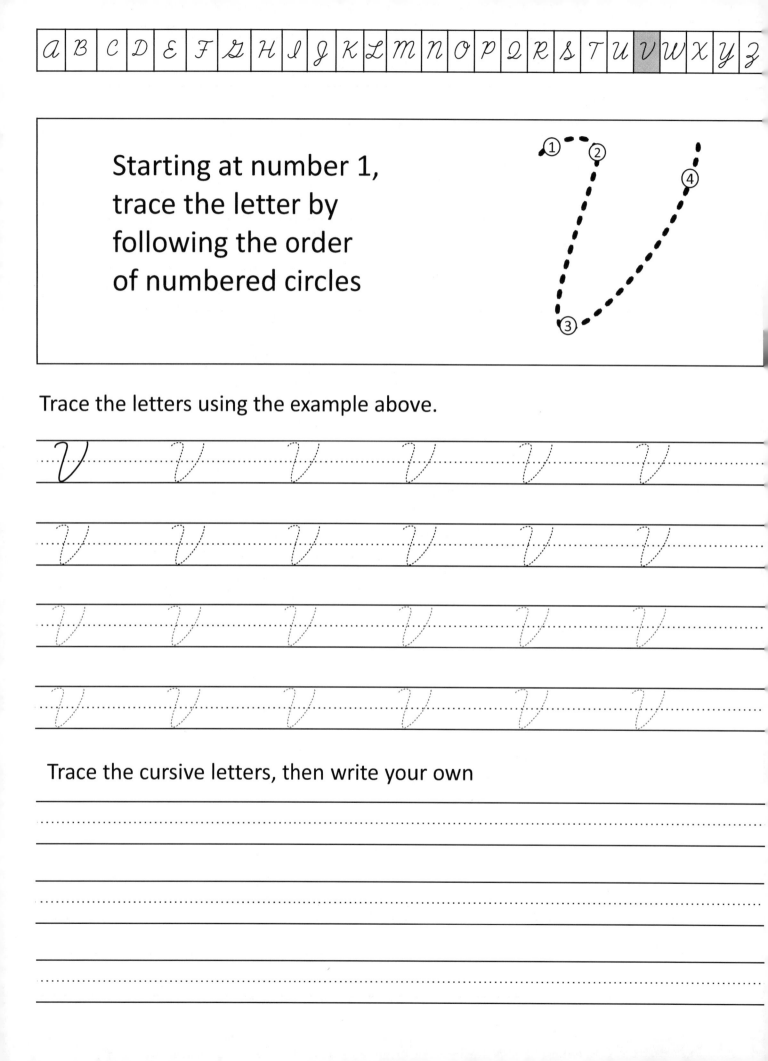

Trace the letters using the example above.

Trace the cursive letters, then write your own

a	b	c	d	e	f	g	h	i	j	k	l	m	n	o	p	q	r	s	t	u	v	w	x	y	z

Starting at number 1, trace the letter by following the order of numbered circles

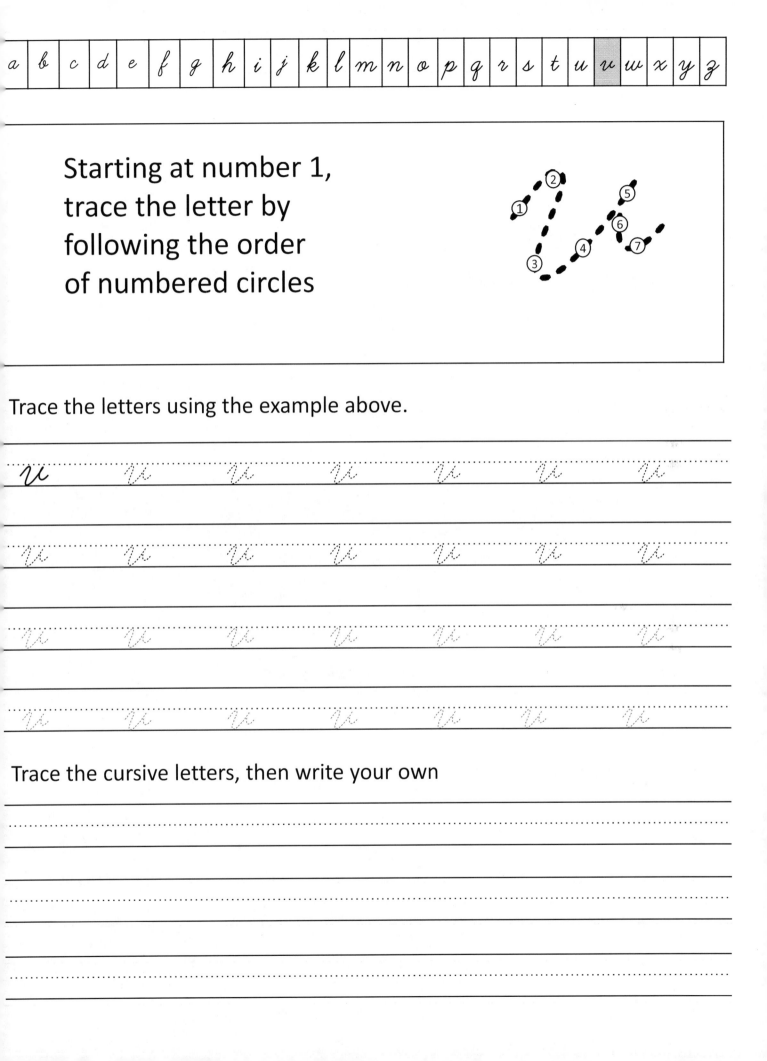

Trace the letters using the example above.

Trace the cursive letters, then write your own

a B C D E F G H I J K L M N O P Q R S T U V W X Y Z

Starting at number 1,
trace the letter by
following the order
of numbered circles

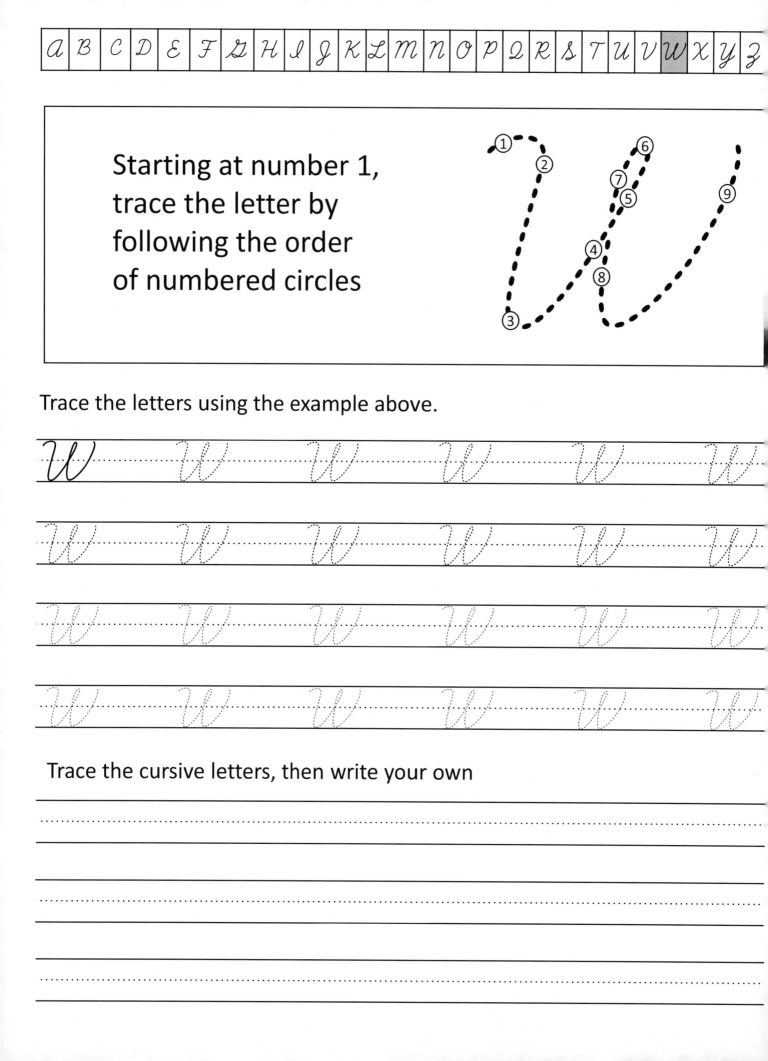

Trace the letters using the example above.

Trace the cursive letters, then write your own

a	b	c	d	e	f	g	h	i	j	k	l	m	n	o	p	q	r	s	t	u	v	w	x	y	z

Starting at number 1, trace the letter by following the order of numbered circles

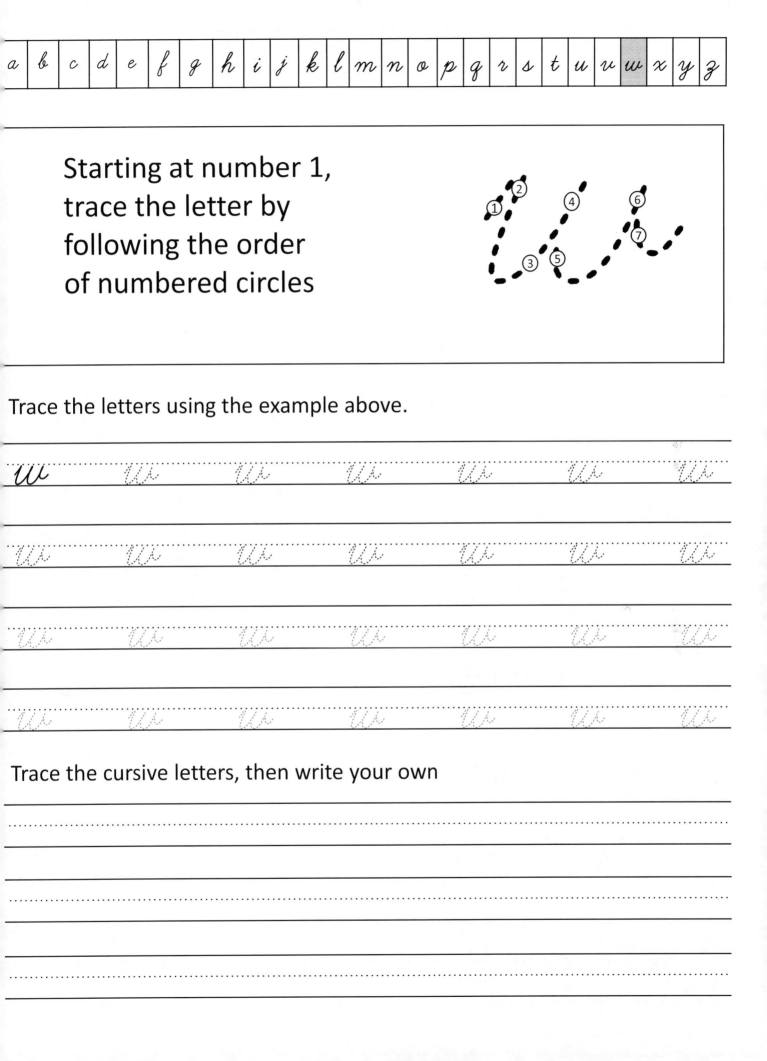

Trace the letters using the example above.

Trace the cursive letters, then write your own

a | B | C | D | E | F | G | H | I | J | K | L | M | N | O | P | Q | R | S | T | U | V | W | X | Y | Z

Starting at number 1,
trace the letter by
following the order
of numbered circles

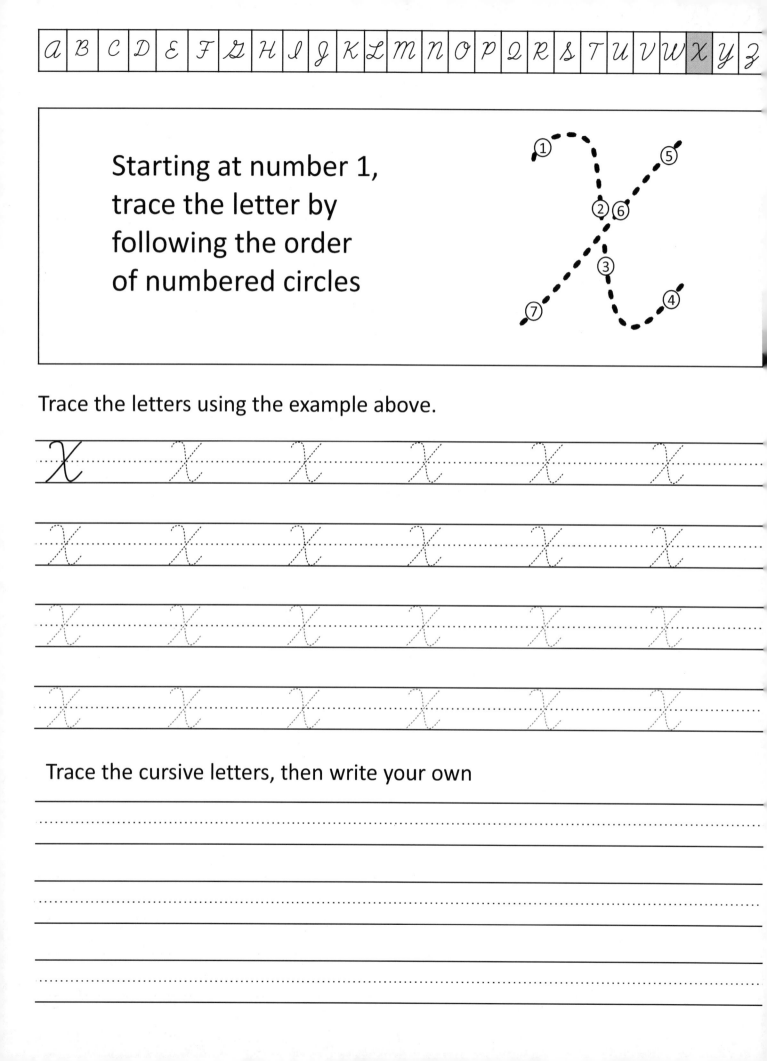

Trace the letters using the example above.

Trace the cursive letters, then write your own

a	b	c	d	e	f	g	h	i	j	k	l	m	n	o	p	q	r	s	t	u	v	w	x	y	z

Starting at number 1,
trace the letter by
following the order
of numbered circles

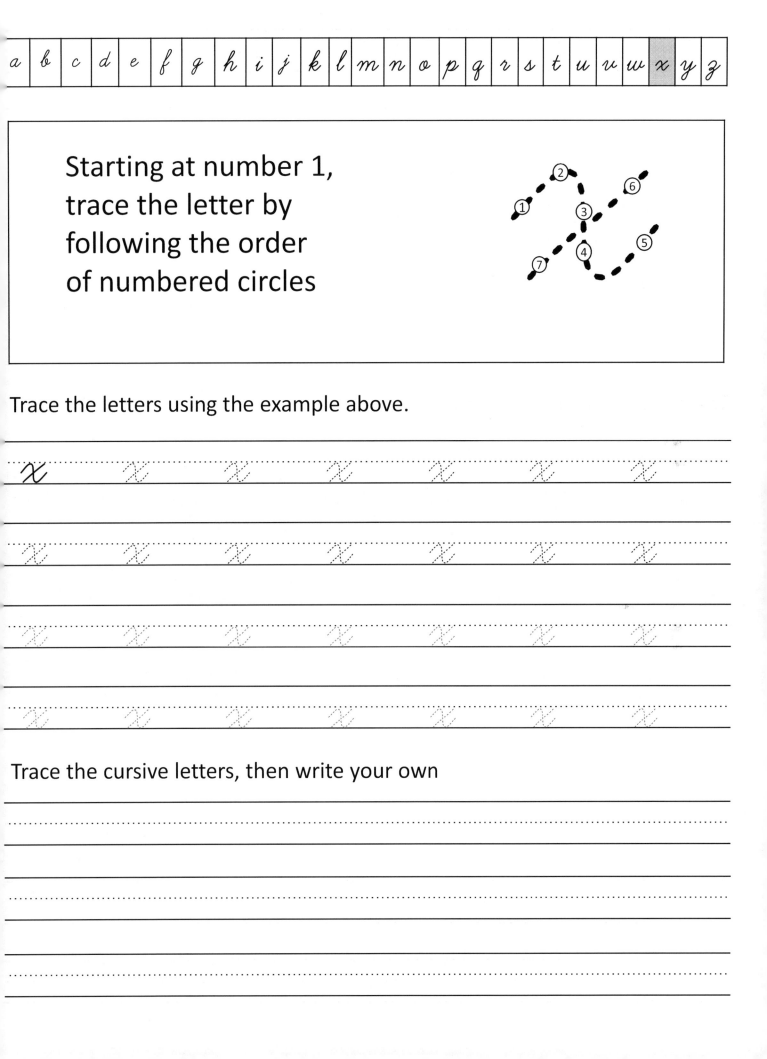

Trace the letters using the example above.

Trace the cursive letters, then write your own

Starting at number 1, trace the letter by following the order of numbered circles

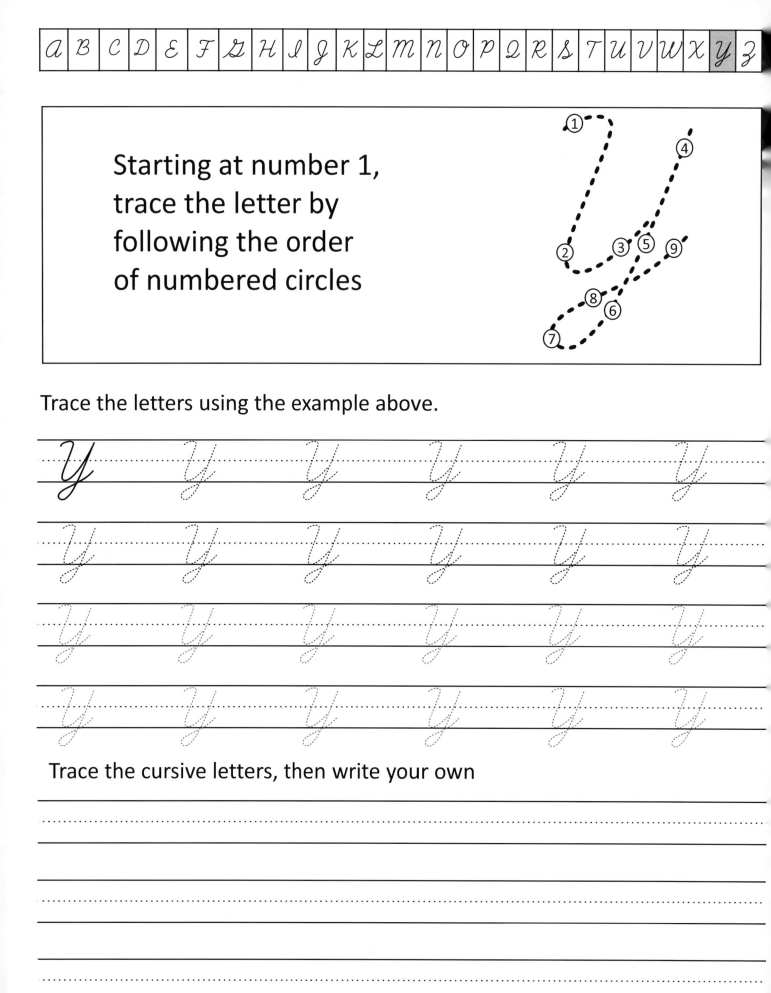

Trace the letters using the example above.

Trace the cursive letters, then write your own

Starting at number 1, trace the letter by following the order of numbered circles

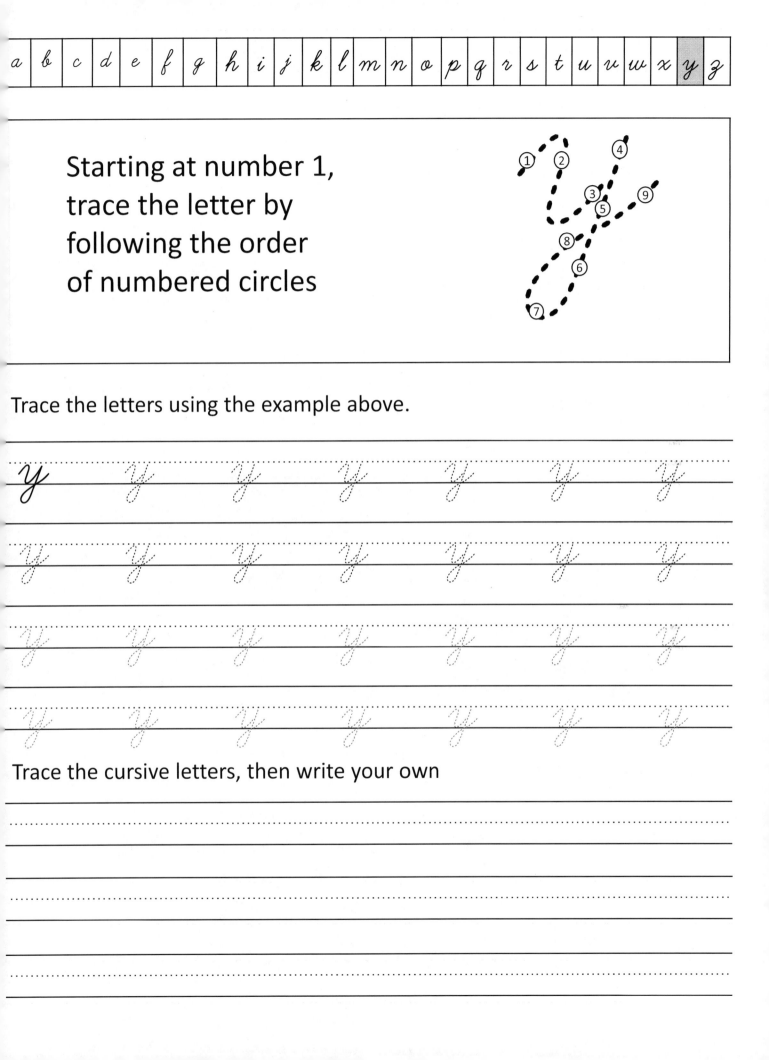

Trace the letters using the example above.

Trace the cursive letters, then write your own

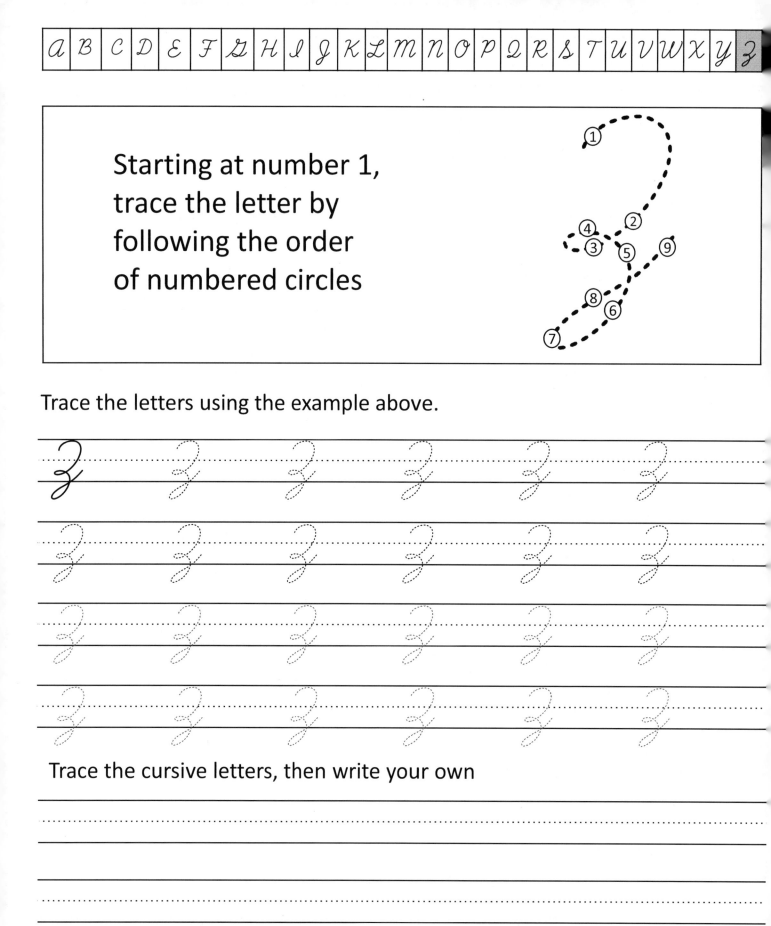

| a | B | C | D | E | F | G | H | I | J | K | L | M | N | O | P | Q | R | S | T | U | V | W | X | Y | Z |

Starting at number 1, trace the letter by following the order of numbered circles

Trace the letters using the example above.

Trace the cursive letters, then write your own

Starting at number 1,
trace the letter by
following the order
of numbered circles

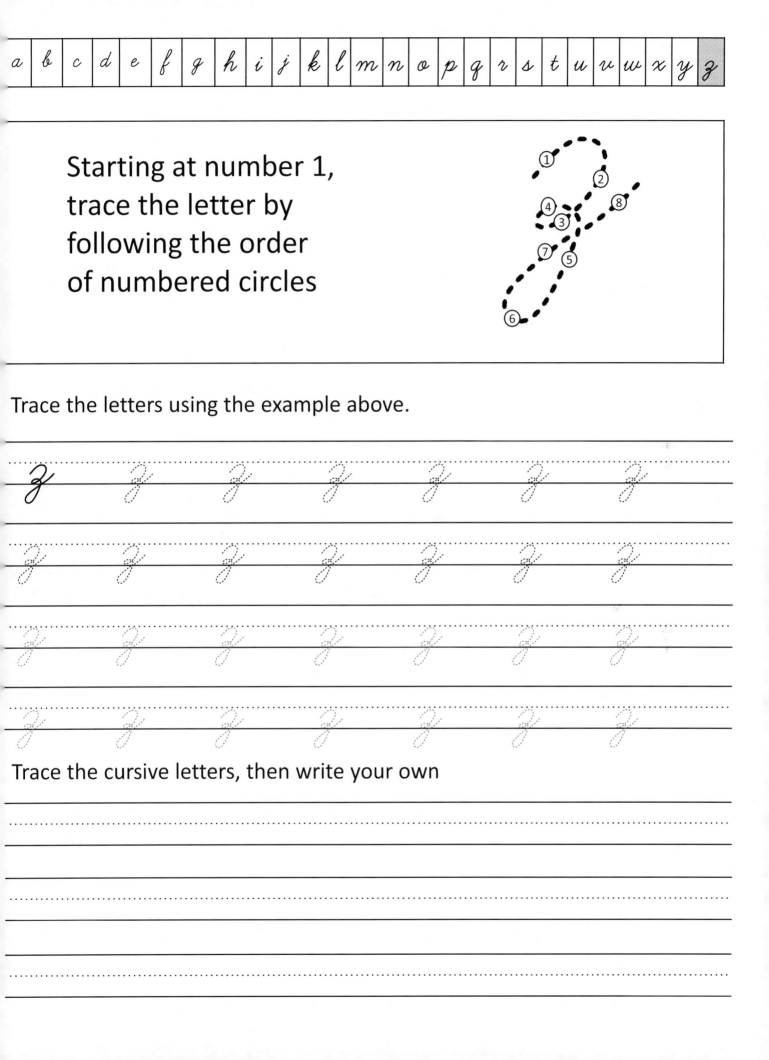

Trace the letters using the example above.

Trace the cursive letters, then write your own

Part 2:
writing three letter words

Are you ready ?
Let's go

all   all   all   all   all

bag   bag   bag   bag   bag

cut   cut   cut   cut   cut

dry   dry   dry   dry   dry

end   end   end   end   end

Write your own words here:

fly fly fly fly fly

got got got got got

hit hit hit hit hit

ice ice ice ice ice ice

joy joy joy joy joy

Write your own words here:

kid   kid   kid   kid   kid

bow   bow   bow   bow   bow

met   met   met   met   met

new   new   new   new   new

own   own   own   own   own

Write your own words here:

pen   pen   pen   pen   pen

red   red   red   red   red

sky   sky   sky   sky   sky

tho   tho   tho   tho   tho

use   use   use   use   use

Write your own words here:

vet vet vet vet vet

why why why why

xd xd xd xd xd xd

yes yes yes yes yes yes

zap zap zap zap zap

Write your own words here:

Part 3:

writing four letter words:

Trace the words and practice writing them in the remaining space

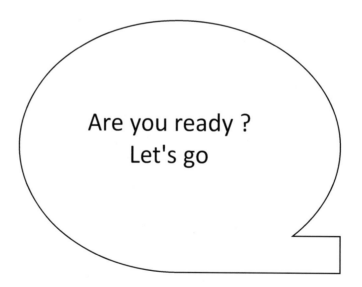

Are you ready ?
Let's go

aged   aged   aged   aged

back   back   back   back

cats   cats   cats   cats

draw   draw   draw   draw

edit   edit   edit   edit   edit

Write your own words here:

fish   fish   fish   fish   fish

gave   gave   gave   gave

hold   hold   hold   hold   hold

idea   idea   idea   idea   idea

just   just   just   just   just

Write your own words here:

keel *keel* *keel* *keel* *keel*

last *last* *last* *last* *last*

more *more* *more* *more* *more*

nigh *nigh* *nigh* *nigh* *nigh*

only *only* *only* *only* *only*

Write your own words here:

peen peen peen peen peen

quip quip quip quip quip

rank rank rank rank rank

vize vize vize vize vize

told told told told told

Write your own words here:

urge *urge* *urge* *urge* *urge*

view *view* *view* *view*

wild *wild* *wild* *wild* *wild*

xmas *xmas* *xmas* *xmas*

your *your* *your* *your* *your*

Write your own words here:

zeal zeal zeal zeal zeal

Part 4:

writing five letter words:

Trace and write the words

Trace the words and practice writing
them in the remaining space

Are you ready ?
Let's go

ablet   ablet   ablet   ablet   ablet

buyer   buyer   buyer   buyer

color   color   color   color   color

depot   depot   depot   depot   depot

earth   earth   earth   earth   earth

Write your own words here:

fable fable fable fable fable

green green green green green

hello hello hello hello hello

ideas ideas ideas ideas ideas

jetty jetty jetty jetty jetty

Write your own words here:

known known known known

later later later later later

money money money money

natty natty natty natty

often often often often often

Write your own words here:

paper paper paper paper paper

quill quill quill quill quill

reset reset reset reset reset

sleep sleep sleep sleep sleep

tolls tolls tolls tolls tolls

Write your own words here:

usual usual usual usual usual

valid valid valid valid valid

women women women women

yeard yeard yeard yeard

zebra zebra zebra zebra zebra

Write your own words here:

Part 5:

writing words starting with a Capital letter:

Connecting uppercase cursive letters A-Z

Are you ready ?
Let's go

Are Are Are Are

Able Able Able

Bus Bus Bus Bus

Ball Ball Ball

Cat Cat Cat Cat

Clock Clock Clock

Did Did Did Did

Dull Dull Dull

Ear Ear Ear Ear

Easy Easy Easy

Write your own words here:

Few Few Few Few

Find Find Find

Go Go Go Go

Girl Girl Girl

Hat Hat Hat Hat

Hard Hard Hard

Info Info Info Info

Invent Invent Invent

Joy Joy Joy Joy

Joint Joint Joint

Write your own words here:

Kid Kid Kid Kid

Know Know Know

Log Log Log Log

Lunch Lunch Lunch

Man Man Man Man

Must Must Must

Now Now Now Now

Night Night Night

On On On On On

Option Option Option

Write your own words here:

Pig Pig Pig Pig

Play Play Play

Quit Quit Quit Quit

Question Question

Rest Rest Rest Rest

Respect Respect Respect

Sun Sun Sun Sun

Seen Seen Seen

Top Top Top Top

Tiger Tiger Tiger

Write your own words here:

Urn Urn Urn Urn

Uncle Uncle Uncle

You You You You

Visit Visit Visit Visit

We We We We

Write Write Write

Xd Xd Xd Xd

Xmas Xmas Xmas

Yes Yes Yes Yes

Year Year Year

Write your own words here:

Zeal Zeal Zeal Zeal

Zebra Zebra Zebra

Part 6:
writing Numbers and Numbers Words 1- 20
Learn and practice Numbers 1-20

Are you ready ?
Let's go

0 0 0 0 0 0 0

zero zero zero zero

1 1 1 1 1 1 1

one one one one

2 2 2 2 2 2 2

two two two two

3 3 3 3 3 3 3

three three three three

4 4 4 4 4 4 4

four four four four

Write your own words here:

5 5 5 5 5 5 5

five five five five

6 6 6 6 6 6 6

six six six six

7 7 7 7 7 7 7

seven seven seven seven

8 8 8 8 8 8 8

eight eight eight eight

9 9 9 9 9 9 9

nine nine nine nine

Write your own words here:

10 10 10 10 10 10

Ten Ten Ten Ten

11 11 11 11 11 11

Eleven Eleven Eleven

12 12 12 12 12 12

Twelve Twelve Twelve

13 13 13 13 13 13

Thirteen Thirteen Thirteen

14 14 14 14 14 14

Fourteen Fourteen Fourteen

Write your own words here:

15 15 15 15 15 15

Fifteen Fifteen Fifteen

16 16 16 16 16 16

Sixteen Sixteen Sixteen

17 17 17 17 17 17

Seventeen Seventeen Seventeen

18 18 18 18 18 18

Eighteen Eighteen Eighteen

Write your own words here:

19   19   19   19   19   19

Nineteen Nineteen Nineteen

20   20   20   20   20   20

Twenty Twenty Twenty Twenty

Days of the week:

Monday Monday Monday

Tuesday Tuesday Tuesday Tuesday

Wednesday Wednesday Wednesday

Thursday Thursday Thursday

Friday Friday Friday Friday

Saturday Saturday Saturday

Sunday Sunday Sunday

months of the year:

January January January

February February February

March March March March

April April April April

May May May May May

June June June June June

July July July July July

August August August August

September September September

October October October October

November November November

December December December

Part 7:

Writing simple sentences and motivational quotes

I can get through anything

I don't need to be perfect

I have courage and confidence

I look on my father as a role
model

I live each day to the fullest

Today, I will walk through my

fears

Today, I chose happiness

You make me smile

Keep up the good work

You are so helpful

I set goal and I reach them

I love and enjoy everything I do

I give my homework priority

I am worthy of greatness

I am a nice person, I treat people
kindly

I brush my teeth after every meal

My life is getting wonderful and
beautiful

I am sure of myself that I will
fulfill my dreams

I appreciate the effort you are
doing for me

If you have succeeded once, you can

train to master better and better

I appreciate the effort you are

doing for me

I get up early, have breakfast, and

go to school active

You are a wonderful person who

can succeed in your life

Tell me how to imagine success

You don't listen to me

I like to travel with my friends

What is your favourite subject?

"The will to succeed is important, but what's more important is the will to prepare." — Bobby Knight

"There is nothing deep down inside us except what we have put there ourselves." — Richard Rorty

"Never retreat. Never explain. Get it done and let them howl."

— Benjamin Jowett

"Appreciation is a wonderful thing. It makes what is excellent in others belong to us as well." — Voltaire

"Quality is not an act, it is a habit"

Aristotle

"I like the dreams of the future

better than the history of the past"

Thomas Jefferson

"Action is the foundational key to all success" Pablo Picasso

"The harder the conflict, the more glorious the triumph" Thomas Paine

"There is nothing like a dream to create the future" Victor Hugo

"The greatest source of happiness is the ability to be grateful at all time." Zig Ziglar

"Do the difficult things while they are easy and do the great things while they are small." Lao Tzu

"The most certain way to succeed is always to try just one more time."

Thomas A. Edison

"Success consists of going from failure to failure without loss of enthusiasm." Winston Churchill

"Happiness lies in the joy of achievement and the thrill of creative effort". Franklin D. Roosevelt

"If you ask me what I came into this life to do, I will tell you: I came to live out loud." Emile Zola

"Moral excellence comes about as a result of habit. We become just by doing just acts, temperate by doing temperate acts, brave by doing brave acts." — Aristotle

"Believe in yourself! Have faith in your abilities! Without a humble but reasonable confidence in your own powers you cannot be successful or happy".

Norman Vincent Peale

Manufactured by Amazon.ca
Bolton, ON

33813352R00061